A M

A MILLION MISSIONS

THE NON-PROFIT SECTOR IN INDIA

MATHEW CHERIAN

First published in India in 2014 by:
Paranjoy Guha Thakurta
paranjoy@gmail.com

Copyright © Mathew Cherian 2014

ISBN 978-93-84439-00-2

Mathew Cherian asserts the moral right to be identified as
the author of this work.

First Edition

Typeset in 11.5/15.5 Adobe Garamond Pro
by Ram Das Lal, NCR Delhi

Printed and bound at
Saurabh Printers
Okhla, New Delhi

Cover design: PealiDezine

Publishing facilitation: AuthorsUpFront

Distribution: FEEL Books

DEDICATION

To my parents Cherian and Sosamma who gave me
a happy childhood and allowed me to pursue my dreams.

The proceeds of this book will be donated to a few non-profits like HelpAge India, Friendicoes, Wildlife SOS and AAM Foundation for their work.

CONTENTS

ACKNOWLEDGEMENTS

How does one thank a million missions? And the dedicated, committed people who have chosen the roads less travelled, who work with scarce resources, frugal means to achieve their dreams of a more just and humane society.

This book would not have been possible without the support of HelpAge India and Amal Ganguli. The manuscript was prepared by Laisa Paul and Meena Takhi who have given their time typing out the first few drafts. I am grateful to Paranjoy Guha Thakurta who saw possibilities in my ramblings. I will also like to thank Vijay Simha and Jyotirmoy Chaudhuri who helped bring the book to its current form.

The book would not have been possible without the inspiration and prodding of my partner Amita Joseph and my children, Aparajita and Arundati.

Mathew Cherian
New Delhi, 1 June 2014

INTRODUCTION

The voluntary sector in India has emerged from the nation's strong traditions of voluntary work (shram daan) and contributions of philanthropy in education (vidya daan). In 1860, the colonial administration wished to regulate civil society and implemented the Societies Registration Act 1860, by which all groups with seven or more members had to be registered. The number of voluntary agencies in India is now over 1.2 million, according to a joint study by Society for Participatory Research in Asia (PRIA), Delhi and the Institute for Policy Studies, Johns Hopkins University, Baltimore, published in 2002.

The voluntary sector is fairly large and encompasses different ideologies, from Gandhian to Marxist thought. Its roots are ancient and deep. Religious philanthropy has shaped generations in India from time immemorial. Much later, the Father of the Nation, Mahatma Gandhi, preached and practiced public service. He was a role model to the vast voluntary sector in India.

While some non-governmental organisations (NGOs) work in remote areas of India bringing relief and succour to millions, others concentrate on articulating the rights of the poor and those displaced from their habitat in order to reduce exploitation by privileged groups, government officials or corporate entities.

In this book we have covered agencies working in a wide spectrum of activities, from children to the arts and culture. The case studies of NGOs doing exceptional work illustrate the range of work being carried out. Many international non-profits have been concerned about the lack of systematic data on the Indian voluntary sector, often due to poor documentation and, in many cases, minimal sharing of data among donor agencies.

In spite of the good work, legislation to curb the sector has grown. The various Acts and tax regulations make it difficult for small NGOs to survive and do good work. Some of the laws are covered in the book, as are the areas where financial resources can be obtained.

The voluntary agencies in India are important, particularly now that the government has been able to earmark substantial funds for that sector. Many of the remote areas and underprivileged sections of society are serviced only by voluntary agencies. I have seen many small agencies working in remote areas with little or no funding.

It intends to promote the much maligned voluntary sector where there is plenty of good work happening unknown, unsung and unheard.

Mathew Cherian
1 June 2014

Chapter 1

BEING GOOD IN INDIA

"Ask nothing; want nothing in return. Give what you have to give; it will come back to you. But do not think of that now, it will come back multiplied a thousand fold. The attention must not be on that. Yet have the power to give; so give willingly. If you wish to help a person, never think what the person's attitude should be towards you."

– Swami Vivekananda

The quest for knowledge began in India thousands of years ago, 6000 BC, from the Harappan civilisation. They had intimate knowledge of the size and shape of bricks. The foundation of geometry to the binomial equations was laid in this period. India's gift to the world of numbers, the numeral zero, has given binary logic and led to the whole wide world of electronic computing. Similarly, philanthropy had its roots in India.

In the Upanishads, daanam, the equivalent of philanthropy (philein + anthropos = love of humankind) in European literature, has been set with cardinal rules. Whenever one donates, they look at 'desh', 'kaal' and 'patra';—the three cardinal principles.

1

This daanam is now ingrained and set in many Indians. Desh is the principle of region in need, where a state or province may be affected by a natural disaster or extreme food shortage. Kaal is the principle of time of need. Every person goes through a cycle of good times and bad times. The Upanishads indicate that one has to practice daanam when people go through bad times. The third principle, patra indicates whether the recipient of daan deserves it. This is in consonance with the principle of accountability where a recipient of charity is accountable to the daan received.

The Upanishads also indicate the gradation of daanam which is shram daan, anna daan, vastra daan and gyan daan. Islam has norms on giving known as Zakat, which is bound by its own governing rules. Along with it is Fidiya which is more like a fine imposed on those violating the fast in the month of Ramadan. Christianity has its rules of tithe which is a tenth of the income to be set aside for charity. This is similar to Sikhism which also has its Dasvandh which translates to a tenth for the poor and disabled.

All religions practiced in India have a commonality in their philanthropic messages and in their lexicon. Where is the divide? Jesus Christ in his sermon says "what you do to the least of them, you do unto me". This has inspired many missionaries to serve the poor irrespective of religion, caste or creed. I have tried to weave the religious philanthropy which drives Indian civil society. In India, early travellers like Tavernier and Ibn Battuta have spoken of several dharamshalas for weary travellers across the country, with hospitality like never experienced before. Truly like Atithi devo bhava (My guest is God). The spirit of giving and sharing runs in the genetic code of many Indians down from the Taittiriya Upanishads which said "Pitru devo bhava, Matru devo bhava, Guru devo bhava, Atithi devo bhava".

The transfer of this knowledge down the generations has led to a greater influence on the country's values and the spiritual lexicon of interconnectedness. The base of voluntarism and volunteering has been built on this tradition. Volunteering or shram daan is seen as an extension of work with your hands which will provide spiritual awakening to the soul. This world of shram daan has been practiced the most in the voluntary sector. Many years ago when I was with Baba Amte, I was woken up early in the morning to plant trees. Even towards the end, when the Baba lay on the banks of the Narmada waiting to be swallowed by the waters of the river, he continued to perform shram daan. I had the good fortune of being with him and planting trees, which the greed of the dam lobby has swallowed and destroyed.

Most non-governmental organisations (NGOs) have small teams, many of whom are volunteers providing their time free, out of sheer commitment to the cause the NGO works for. This is particularly so in rural areas where many volunteers are still engaged in agricultural operations and give part of their time to working for the NGO. In urban centres, most volunteers are middle-class and upper-class women. NGO activities that attract volunteers are related to programmes such as crisis prevention, mental health, relief for the elderly and for young children, AIDS prevention and counselling for teenagers. NGOs that are more oriented to service delivery generally rely on part- or full-time staff.

In the absence of clear statistics, it is difficult to estimate the number of volunteers and staff of the NGO sector as a whole. Nevertheless, this is a growing field in which cultural traditions have made voluntary work an integral part of family life. A major challenge is to channelise the energies and capacities of the volunteers effectively, and enable them to give their best without the hazards of commuting long distances or wasting time in inefficient or irrelevant tasks.

The earliest estimate was given by a PRIA-Johns Hopkins study in 2002 that said there were 1.2 million NGOs in India. Subsequently, the ebullient Dr Pronab Sen, Secretary in the Ministry of Statistics and Programme Implementation (MSPI), carried out a survey in 2010 (MSPI, 2012) and estimated that there were approximately 3.2 million non-profit institutions (NPIs) in India. The report draws on an ambitious survey implemented in two phases. In the first phase, a comprehensive list of societies was prepared from the Registrar of Societies in each state. The second phase involved physical verification of these societies, and collection of financial and employment data. The report took six years.

The first phase of the survey identified about 3.17 million NPIs registered under the Societies Registration Act, 1860, and the Bombay Public Trusts Act, 1950; 58.7 per cent of these were located in rural areas. The majority of NPIs were engaged in community, social and personal services, cultural services, and education and health services. Subsequently, in the second phase, these listed societies were physically surveyed. Nearly 2.2 million societies, that is 71 per cent of the registered societies were visited, but final survey results were obtained for just 694,000, or 22 per cent. In Andhra Pradesh, barely 15 per cent of the 434,000 NPIs identified in the Phase-I survey could be traced, while in Tamil Nadu about 70 per cent of the NPIs were not traceable. While some had shifted their address, others existed as paper organisations, possibly registered to extract funds from government agencies. Thus, for nearly four-fifths of all societies, we don't know whether they exist (there is no provision for de-registering defunct societies), whether they do anything and, if not, why they exist.

In most states, the provision of submitting financial statements is not enforced. Many of the NPIs traced had poor employment and financial records and, even if they did, often refused to furnish audited accounts, especially if they did not receive funds from statutory bodies. Even if the societies file financial statements with the registrar's office, there is no mechanism to maintain this database, a sad commentary on the quality of statistics at the state level.

Despite these limitations, the report sheds much-needed light on this sector. Three activities social services (37 per cent), education and research (24 per cent), and culture and recreation (15 per cent) account for 76 per cent of the traced societies. The number of NPIs reporting religion as their primary activity is surprisingly low less than five per cent say so (down from 18.4 per cent in 1970). Nearly 80 per cent of the traced societies were formed after 1990, and just three per cent before 1970. The total workforce of 18.2 million workers exceeds the entire public sector workforce. However, only 2.7 million are paid workers (the rest are volunteers). Surprisingly, female workers in these societies make up just 28 per cent, not much higher than in the non-agriculture workforce in general.

With regard to finances, 54 per cent of the funds of these societies come from grants, while 16 per cent comes from donations and offerings, and 16 per cent from income. Nearly half the funds are deployed for education, followed by social services (20 per cent) and health (11 per cent). While half the expenditure is incurred on the purchase of goods and services, wages and salary account for 28 per cent.

The survey divides these NPIs into three groups: those whose activities are largely financed through government aid and grants (societies serving government); professional associations, chambers of commerce and so on, which serve the common interests of their members (societies serving industries); and societies that provide goods or services to households and are not mainly financed by the government (societies serving households). The last category includes religious societies, clubs, trade and labour unions, resident welfare associations and so on. Societies serving households make up 89 per cent; eight per cent and three per cent serve the government and industries, respectively. Nearly two-thirds of the total funds (₹72,792 crore) are used by societies serving households; 32 per cent by societies serving government. About half the funds go towards education and research, and just under three per cent for religion.

Assuming a third of them do not work, there are still a million non-profits in the voluntary sector. All of them work on their individual missions, which add up to a million missions. This has the power to transform India in myriad ways. All of them are doing good work and in their own way changing India the way the Mahatma wanted.

Voluntary sector in India

Voluntary associations were not new to India or Pakistan. Religious movements had for many centuries drawn individuals to them on the basis of belief rather than birth. The British-Indian government also strengthened this type of organisation through laws granting legal recognition to associations that registered with it. This, in turn, gave them legal rights to own property and to conduct business, sabhas, anjumans and samajes (samitis) spring up in all religious communities with constitutions, bylaws, office-bearers, annual reports, auditors and statutory accounts—in short the organisation structure adopted by British charities. The societies purchased property, built places of worship, ran schools, orphanages, hospitals and old age homes. They also ran farms for aged cows, hospitals, dispensaries, reading rooms, libraries and other charitable activities. They bought printing presses and issued their own newsletters, journals, tracts and books. These organisations also created impressive financial systems and sophisticated forms of fundraising that enabled them to maintain and expand the variety of charitable institutions they forwarded. Their contribution to civil society is amazing but little positive is written about them. The associations draw inspiration from religion and the philanthropic traditions in the subcontinent.

The Ramakrishna Math and Mission at Belur, started by Ramakrishna Paramahansa (born Gadadhar Chatterjee) and his wife Ma Sarada Devi with its systems of hospitals and dispensaries, and its extensive relief projects, is one of the early voluntary agencies still continuing its good work across India.

The Dayanand Anglo-Vedic Society (commonly referred to as DAV Society) is from the Arya Samaj (Noble Society) which brought to Hinduism a system of proselytism with professional missionaries. In 1874 Swami Dayananda travelled to Gujarat and Bombay [now Mumbai]. On 10 April 1874 he established the Bombay Arya Samaj. It was one of the first successful societies he established. Lala Hans Raj was involved in the formation of the Lahore Arya Samaj. Lala Hans Raj, a Bhalla Khatri, had joined the Arya Samaj while a student of the Lahore Government College. His act of selflessness rekindled the desire for a school. The newly organised Dayanand Anglo-Vedic Trust and Management Society held its first meeting on 17 February 1886 and the school was opened on 1 June 1886. The Dayanand Anglo-Vedic Trust and Management Society was the first centralising organisation within the Samaj with representatives from many branches. In 1877 Rai

Mathura Das started the first Arya Samaj orphanage in Ferozepur. It grew slowly until the famines of the late 1890s. Lala Lajpat Rai, a leading moderate in the Arya Samaj, announced that the Samaj would shelter any orphan sent to them. In February 1897 he began a campaign to collect funds for orphan relief. Lala Lajpat Rai was first a social worker and established the Servants of People Society (now located at Lajpat Bhavan, near Lajpat Nagar, New Delhi).

Orphan and famine relief illustrate the view of the Hindus in those days, especially of the moderate Arya Samaj members. The DAV Societies have continued this fine tradition and have established schools and colleges which are centres of excellence in India. There were groups which created model towns in Agra (Dayal Bagh), Beas and Auroville, Pondicherry [now Puducherry]. The Radha Soami Satsang transformed their religious centres into model religious towns at Beas, Agra and they run universities of great repute. The Beas Satsang rested on the foundation laid by Jaimal Singh before his death on 29 December 1903. He was succeeded by Baba Sawan Singh Grewal who remained head of the Beas Satsang until his death in 1948. As with Jaimal Singh, he also served in the military specifically as a senior engineer in the Military Engineering Service. Baba Grewal attracted former soldiers during his career and initiated 124,000 devotees into the Satsang. This was a movement which brought retired army men into voluntary service. Dera Beas became the organisational headquarters for the Beas Radha Soamis.

Meanwhile the Agra branch claimed that Shiv Dayal was a Paramatma Satguru (Supreme Saint), unique in human history. Madhava Prasad became the guru of the Soami Bagh Radha Soamis and took the title of Babuji Maharaj. He held this office until his death in October 1949. Dayal Bagh was transformed into a religious community, the headquarters of an expanding movement. After

Independence, both the Radha Soami Beas Satsang and the Radha Soami Dayal Bagh have developed across the country and have millions of volunteers who work in education and run universities, colleges and schools.

Down south, Shri Aurobindo Ghose inspired the formation of the Aurobindo Society and also inspired several people to begin work to create a new India. Shri Aurobindo said: "Our endeavour shall be to prepare the path and to accomplish the beginning of a great and high change which we believe to be and aim at making the future of the race and the future of India." Shri Aurobindo began with the freedom movement and then realised that the spiritual path is needed for the development of India. Ultimately, Mahatma Gandhi began work on development in Sewagram Ashram in Wardha inspiring several voluntary leaders in India. This laid the foundation for civil society in independent India.

Father of the nation

"He who gives all his time to the service of the people, his whole life is an unbroken round of prayer," wrote Mahatma Gandhi in *Harijan*, on 10 November 1946.

Mahatma Gandhi had planned the 1948 conference in Sewagram, Wardha. This plan was the outcome of his watching, over a long period of time, the evolution of the political and social situation. It was also the outcome of his observing the working of the political class in India in the months leading to Independence and the weeks immediately after political power had been transferred to Indian hands. His last will and testament, in which he proposed the disbanding of the Congress and its transformation into a Lok Seva Sangh, was announced at this conference.

The Mahatma had become convinced that political formations

and personalities were becoming self-absorbed and were moving away from serving public interest. His fear, expressed in his work *Hind Swaraj* (1909) that home rule without swaraj would only mean the replacement of the tiger (the British) by another (our own), was active once again in his mind. In the weeks after Independence, Gandhi seemed to be convinced that India's political and social development would become reality only with swaraj, self-rule.

Gandhi's last message was that in a free society, political parties must regard politics to be a form of public service rather than a means to dominate fellow citizens. And the Mahatma wanted to take this forward with the same force that he had applied to the political field. The Sewagram meeting was to have embodied that drive. On 30 January 1948, three bullets stopped Mohandas Karamchand Gandhi as he walked to a public prayer on the lawns of Birla House, New Delhi. His philosopher grandson Ramchandra Gandhi, then aged eleven, put it differently several years later when he said "Gandhi stopped three bullets on their deathly trajectory of hate".

His assassin, as a result, did great disservice not only to political India but also to the founding of a new moral and just order in the country, and also for humankind.

Sewagram (Wardha), March 1948—A historic meeting

Six weeks after Gandhi's assassination, a few men and women gathered at Sevagram to search their hearts and their mind for answers. They included Congress president Rajendra Prasad, Acharya Kripalani, Jayaprakash Narayan, Vinobha Bhave, JC Kumarappa, Kamalnayan Bajaj, Maulana Abul Kalam Azad, and Jawaharlal Nehru (who joined two days later) among many others. Out of this deliberation emerged the Sarva Seva Sangh (SSS)—

the first of its kind—a voluntary agency in Independent India. The mandate was to carry forward the Mahatma's plan to build a casteless society based on truth and nonviolence in which every individual and group gets full opportunity to develop to the best of their potential.

This mandate of the Mahatma inspires the voluntary sector across India, which is close to a million active NGOs. Or, a million missions. The Sarvodaya Samaj set up in March 1948 was the forerunner of many NGOs built by inspirational leaders across India. Very little is written about them. They are not known in the media. The Sarvodaya Samaj became the Akhil Bharatiya Sarva Seva Sangh in 1948. The words Akhil Bharat were dropped in 1965 to become the Sarva Seva Sangh. Many commonly refer to this movement as the Sarvodaya movement. ASSEFA (Association for Sarva Seva Farms), SEWA (Self Employed Women's Association), Gandhi Peace Foundation and Ekta Parishad are part of this glorious radition born in 1948. This laid the foundation for civil society in post-independent India. Jayaprakash Narayan or JP, who also spoke here, later came to be known as Lok Nayak or the people's leader, his movement against the Emergency and authoritarian rule inspiring many other NGOs around the year 1975. Lok Nayak Jayaprakash Narayan wanted Sampoorna Kranti or total revolution. Tarun Bharat Sangh and its founder Rajendra Singh was one of his followers. A famous Magsaysay Award winner, he is known as India's waterman, and established a water revolution. This NGO was part of the great tradition established by JP followers. Gandhi's message had spread to India through its voluntary agencies. They did not see him but they have imbibed his spirit to "wipe every tear from every Indian".

Chapter 2

EARLY ORIGINS IN RELIGIOUS PHILANTHROPY

"Sabaar opore maanush satya" (The supreme truth is humankind)

– Swami Vivekananda

Voluntary action in India is a long-standing tradition. Today's non-governmental sector has many direct links with recent history, in particular the social reform movements of the nineteenth century. The following is a brief outline of the different phases of its evolution.

Early nineteenth century

The first half of the nineteenth century in Indian history was marked by the initiation and rise of social reform movements. This was precipitated in part by the introduction of Western ideas and the Christian faith towards the end of the eighteenth century. The Charter Act of 1813 removed restrictions on Christian missionary activities in India and provided for the maintenance and support of a Church establishment in British India.

Voices were raised by the social reform movements against discrimination by birth and gender. The formation of Atmiya Sabha in 1815 by Raja Ram Mohan Roy was one such example; later it allied with the Christian Unitarians and started the Unitarian Committee in 1821. Brahmin Sabha was established in 1828. Swami Sahajanand's Swaminarayan sect (1800) and Manohar Dharm Sabha (1844) of Gujarat, Paramhans Sabha, Prarthana Sabha, Kalyanonnayak Samaj and Hindu Dharm Sabha in Maharashtra had similar concerns. Many literary educational institutions such as the Royal Asiatic Society (1834) and Dhyan Prakash Sabha (1840) were also founded. The Faradi movement of Haji Shariatullah, founded in 1818 among the economically backward classes of Muslims, reflected similar concerns in the context of Islam.

The spirit evoked by these reform movements inspired many people to engage in activities for the welfare of others less fortunate than themselves.

Late nineteenth century, the reformist phase

The trends of the first phase were consolidated in the latter half of the nineteenth century in institutionalised movements: Brahmo Samaj (by the end of 1878, 124 branches and 21 periodicals had been established in India); Arya Samaj (1875); Ramakrishna Mission (1898); Satyashodhak Samaj (1873); Indian National Social Conference (1887); and Bombay Presidency Social Reform Association (1897). The outreach of these movements had transcended the linguistic and administrative boundaries of their origins.

At the same time, purely political organisations with a limited programme started to emerge (e.g., Pune Sarvajanik Sabha in Maharashtra and British Indian Association in Calcutta).

Literary and educational societies and associations also became a widespread phenomenon, which prompted the British rulers to enact the Societies Registration Act of 1860. The spread of such literary associations contributed to the development of an influential vernacular press and the beginnings of alternative (nationalist) education.

Another feature of the period was the emergence of working class organisations (for example, the Bombay Association of Textile Workers). In 1885, in this sociopolitical environment, the Indian National Congress became an official platform for the expression of growing national consciousness. The typical non-governmental organisations (NGOs) in this period, across the country, were literary and educational societies. All of them were based on religious principles and inspired by faith. Some call it religious philanthropy and some describe it as faith-based philanthropy.

Philanthropy, though not a term or concept of recent vintage, properly finds its current resonance in the new humanism of eighteenth and nineteenth century Europe. This is a spirit that had its genesis under well-known historical and political circumstances, and found its way to distant shores via concurrently generated systems of transmission and propagation, like the modem education system that was so integral to the colonial project in India. It interacted with older thought and belief systems everywhere it reached, leaving in its wake social ideals that were significantly modified, one way or the other, or a string of new hybrid strains. In truth, there was nothing extravagantly novel in this new formulation at the level of idea, except for emphasis on the human in all experience. This merely reflected the new conceptual confidence accompanying the new age (the development of the various human sciences announcing this mini-cognitive revolution).

Philein + anthropos = to love man. This equation—if one overlooks the fact that a fellow feeling towards humankind expresses, at least in part, a religious attitude—can be seen to find validation in a modern, rationally-ordered world where it has replaced the love of god as a guiding principle of existence. Religious philanthropy, in that sense, would seem to be a notion tainted by anachronism. But, as a group of activities, it has only gained in size and strength. Not only that, it has also updated its mode of operations at one level to a corporatised level of efficiency and scale, and at another to bring it in tune with contemporary trends in development-oriented voluntarism. For these reasons, it is a phenomenon that deserves study both as a powerful actor on the social stage and, in itself, as an interesting ideological complex of modem political notions and more traditional impulses.

In as much as the phrase religious philanthropy is clearly composed of two components, it bifurcates and deflects inquiry into two distinct but interloping levels of human experience and reality. One is the theological level, the domain that articulates the situation of man in a whole cosmology, one that is arranged according to theocentric principles, that is, dominated by and deriving from the Godhead; and which, in laying out this situation, places man in a network of relations with the theocentrics at one end and with fellow beings at the other. This level directs us to a study of the scriptural or doctrinal basis of a belief system where such is available, or to other productions of cultural groups (myths, manifestoes, etc.) that express this set of relations.

The other relates to a more tangible, sociological level: the question of existing in practical communion with the rest of humankind, the boundaries between what is public and what is private, that is, the actual domain where the issue of sharing crops up. This involves sketching out of the nature of social relations that obtains at a given place and time, its evolution and trajectory. And, since philanthropy mostly takes the shape of material help, also the underlying economic bases for such interaction.

Given that the two domains operate at entirely separate levels of motivation, the possibility of overlap being logically equal to the potential for mismatch or outright opposition, one can say that religious philanthropy is an act that is realisable only when the two domains interact positively. Or, to put it differently, one could say that enabling conditions must exist at two distinct layers of life for such acts to take place.

The Indian situation

To transport this set of issues to India is to bring in a mélange of uniquely Indian problems: an open-ended, constantly evolving and synthesising system, the absence of a single doctrinaire text that imposes a fixed charter of demands or a regulatory code of behaviour and action, heterogeneity of an extreme order along geographical, ethnic, social axes, a complex historical trajectory with many interweaving elements, a multitude of attitudes even within so-called closed systems. With all this, common strains can still be discerned both within particular Indian systems and in the problems that have arisen in seeing and defining them. The first problem can be posed thus: can there be a specific Indian philanthropy; or what place does the cluster of notions that philanthropy invokes have in a loosely-defined Indian reality? In the individualised nature of relationship that is allowed for between man and his creator in Indian belief systems, it would appear, prima facie, that the notion of community can be granted existence only at a subsidiary order of reality. It would follow of necessity that the idea of philanthropy as a primary human impulse does not entirely sit well with an Indian (Hindu) worldview that places emphasis on a sort of personal contract with God, the terms of which are open to be fulfilled by whatever mode is available or deemed desirable. Even accounts at the level of popular transmission and understanding put across a view roughly like this: each living creature is a fragment of divinity, estranged from the godhead for the duration of the cycle of birth and rebirth; and each is alone in the quest for regaining that lost wholeness. All else is illusory, a blurry tedium of responsibilities that have to borne because they come attached with this teleological apparatus, a great ocean of apparitions that is there only to be crossed. The obvious question is: where does one locate a social conscience (or even consciousness) within this?

HINDU PHILANTHROPY

The task of characterising an essentially Hindu philanthropy has to wrestle with a basic problematic—that is, how to draw a consistent model from its theological roots that will fit easily onto the plane of action, whether seen historically or in the modern context. How to reconcile the notion of the immanence of God in every item of creation—animate and inanimate—with the seeming lack of an egalitarian ideal in social organisation, with what must be the most elaborate and evolved theoretical defence of social stratification in the history of man, indeed the very apotheosis of hierarchy. Given that oppositions of the most extreme order (say, from polytheism to atheism; from idolatry to the nirguna) coexist in this apparently seamless web of ideologies, and doctrinal justification can be discovered within it for any imaginable breed of worldview, a more complete exercise will have to correlate it with the actual social reality and its own guiding laws. Implicated in such an exercise, however, is also the unavoidable fact that it tends to conduct an appraisal of historical situations with a retrospective application of modern standards: what calls for most vigil is a loose orientalist characterisation of the Hindu worldview as one that comes closest to defeatism or one that disengages action from a temporally verifiable cause-and-effect relation with its consequences to such a degree that it seems to insist on the pointlessness of action. If everyone is alone, and deeds have only a cumulative effect at some distant point in one's personal journey, is there scope for immediately meaningful social intervention, one that engages with the present in order to effect changes in the very basis of institutionalised inequality?

A study of philanthropy in this latter, modern sense—rather than in the older sense of ritualised charity—not only has to tread this ideological minefield, it must simultaneously understand the imperatives that brought about qualitative changes in the way Hindu society looked at itself, especially during and after the colonial encounter. Add to that the question of tracing in its historical movement the many philosophical breaks—which successfully radicalised certain groups of ideas—and the equally numerous co-options (e.g., Buddhism and Advaita). There also exist the fuzzy boundaries with the adivasi systems that predated a stabilised varna categorisation their proto-democratic character and strong concept of a shared participation in economy, with a conspicuous absence of private property, are said to have been influential on Buddhism; whereas their animist beliefs centered around a sense of the interconnectedness of all things were absorbed in toto by mainstream religion.

Overall, one can delineate an uneven line of evolution—partly autonomous, partly influenced by extraneous streams—from the early Vedic culture to the classical civilisation built around the Laws of Manu that stressed religious giving; through the egalitarian products of the many reformist upsurges (first the Jaina and Buddha streams, then the medieval Bhakti movement that intermingled with Islamic components to produce Sufism and Sikhisim); to those that arose out of contact with the modern Enlightenment project, combining revivalism with reform (Brahmo Samaj, Arya Samaj, Ramakrishna Mission); latter day variants of the spirit of nationalism and voluntarism like the Rastriya Swayamsevak Sangh (RSS); up to the huge modern cults that have formed around godmen (such as the Puttaparthi Saibaba and Mata Amritanandamayi). The question of which one finally has a fixed identity separate from Hinduism need not concern us here: what is relevant is that all elements have influenced one another in their interplay over centuries to such a degree that the more distant entities may possess commonalities and the more seemingly Hindu ones may have unsuspectingly internalised outer influences.

Contexts of giving

"What politics is to Europe, religion is to India." When Vivekananda said this, he had already seen the whole of India and most of the West. He knew that dharma in India referred to that essential, universal spirit behind sects-not sectarian beliefs. He believed that only those programmes for social change will have a lasting effect that takes into account the fact that dharma is the central theme of our national existence. The word itself, often peddled as a synonym for religion, has in fact a wider sense encompassing eternal law and social morality that cannot be captured easily in the more fixed, Semitic sense of religion that dominates today. But as a spirit that can be said to percolate India's philosophy, literature, arts, and science, music, sculpture, architecture, civic life, commerce, politics, customs, rituals, it sets up an overarching framework in which all such transactions can happen. The freedom struggle is a clear example. Neither was it simply a social nor a political reform movement; it had an essential core of certain ethical values. First and foremost, it appealed to the moral nature of human beings, cutting across all party lines; only then did it offer a social or political agenda for action. It is within this scheme of interconnectedness that one can apprehend traditional notions like daana, charity, the greatest of all virtues.

Traditional wisdom does not confer birthrights on Hindus, only birthduties towards the gods, the sages, the ancestors and fellowcreaturesdenoted by the corresponding acts of worship, shiksha, ritual and charity (Klostermaier, 2000). The extended Hindu family system of yore also emphasised a communal corpus of wealth, much like that of a socialist state, rather than individual accumulation. A distributive mechanism established within the home is meant as precursor to a similar model to be deployed in relation to the world at large. The Danastuti in the Rig Veda warns, "In vain does the mean man acquire food; It is, I speak the truth, verily his death. He who does not cherish a comrade or a friend! Who eats all alone, is all sin." The codification of daana in the Dharmasastras exhibits traits common to many traditions, specifying the conditions under which transfer of ownership could be said to constitute charity. In some readings, the gift of vidya is considered the greatest a man can make.

The initial theorising on charity gave way to more institutional forms—the king engaged in building public works like dharamshalas, and the rich trader class emulating such acts. A crisis of society developed with the arrival of the Christian missionary on the Indian landscape with his evolved apparatus of charitable mission work. The form of monastic organisation, the new areas of activity in education and health that supplanted older religious giving, the business—like focus and calibrated scale—all this was to have a profound impact on the psyche of the educated Indian. So, along with scanning of the ancient literature for ideological support, a modern type of Indian organisation arose imitating the European one in form and content. The earliest products of the encounter with Europe-like Brahmo Samaj, Arya Samaj and Ramakrishna Mission are typically reformist in intent and already imbued with a seminal nationalism in the sense of being considered and highly self-conscious reactions to the West. But out of these grew a modern philanthropic commitment the likes of which could not be envisaged under the personalised charity of old. The entire voluntary sector in India is based on religious philanthropy and how the early founders used their respective religions to propagate their vision and missions. It is not entirely Hindu but based on Islamic, Christian and Sikh philanthropy. A study of some organisations will help in this understanding.

Hindu Philanthropic Organisations

I have taken up a few organisations whose activities could be said to broadly answer to the description Hindu philanthropy. These are: the Ramakrishna Mission, the Chinmaya Mission, the Tirumala Tirupati Devasthanams and the Jnana Prabodhini. In characterising them, we trace the source of motivation, the chosen domains of activity, the structure and management, and the funding pattern-blending the picture that emerges from field studies, interviews and through their own testimonies. These missions also reflect the genetic makeup of civil society in the country.

In many ways, all four—individually and cumulatively, along with many others in the field—can be said to have extended the existing way of doing philanthropy and created a space that did not exist before in the context of traditional Hindu giving. In this, they are all typically modern, either by inspiration, ideal, or circumstance. It is not coincidental that even in their primary domain of existence as organisations devoted to spiritualism both the Ramakrishna and Chinmaya Missions faced problems of categorisation. For well over half-a-century, members of the Ramakrishna Mission were not accepted as true sanyasis by traditional Hindu orders. And Chinmayananda faced a hostile reception to his initial irreverence in holding free discourses on Vedanta to any member of the laity that evinced interest.

Initiators of a new style of self-reflective thought that is at once revivalist and modern, the Ramakrishna Mission has more than a trace of similarity with the liberal modernist institutions that cropped up on the side of Islamic philanthropy coterminously or later in its avowed secular stance, and found a natural reservoir of support in the educated middle-class, and in its areas of activity. These, on both sides of the religious divide, closely mirror traditional organised Christian activity—health, education, etc., but tie these to their own brands of bedrock liberal spiritualism as the basis.

The Chinmaya Mission and Jnana Prabodhini share this liberalism but, in so far as they crop up chronologically in the next half-century or so, they exhibit features more typical of their time in what goads them to activity. They differ importantly, though, in that one (Chinmaya) can be seen as a personal conquering of a social anomie and cultural neurosis characteristic of rapidly modernising societies. The other though also deriving from one man's vision emanates as a primarily collective, political response to the post-

Independence crisis in Indian society. Both are, equally, children of a historically produced consciousness of nationalism and identity.

The spiritual solution Chinmayananda found to the crisis aligns his Mission with the latter day, new-age cults except that its activities go much beyond. He started with a popularised form of practical Vedanta his Mission, though diversifying into health and education like Ramakrishna Mission, evolved into more modern, networked forms of rural development and advocacy work. The consciousness they concomitantly seek to generate in their target groups, spiritual and nationalist, keep them within the ambit of philanthropy for the sake of a larger cause.

The fourth case, Tirumala Tirupati Devasthanams, is self-avowedly a belated entrant in such organised, modern philanthropy and is motivated by a realisation that its vast corpus of funds can be diverted for useful, productive purposes that can be associated with the trust's name—an almost corporate-style concern with social marketing and public relations. It is traditional, orthodox Hinduism, hitherto satisfied with ritual acts of charity and pilgrim welfare, that can be seen to have been influenced more by historical circumstance and the example of others rather than any deep auto-motivation.

I. The Ramakrishna Mission

It was in the latter half of the nineteenth century, in the reformist ferment brought about by washing up of European ideals on the waning tide of the Bhakti age, that the conditions were set for the birth of the Mission, the largest and oldest institution of its type in India.

Ramakrishna Paramahansa led a life devoted to the contemplation of the divine, abjuring even the Brahmo Samaj ideal of an engaged ethics. It required a philosophical turn of some dexterity on the part of Swami Vivekananda to reorient such asceticism towards practical Vedanta and the figure of Daridra Narayan, Lord Vishnu in the shape of a beggar—in short, an apotheosis of the poor Indian, with the pithy, persuasive motto, nar seva, narayan seva. Thus was born a modern movement anchored in a re-reading of the old texts, wedded to the national impulse and yet universalist in its insistence upon the oneness of existence, the divinity of man and the fundamental unity of all systems of thought.

The mystic Ramakrishna was born on 19 February 1836 in a village in Hooghly district of present day West Bengal and eventually settled as a priest at Dakshineswar temple, founded in 1855 by Rani Rashmoni of Calcutta. In between total immersion in devotion, he came in contact with the intellectual leadership of Bengal, figures like Keshub Chandra Sen, Iswarchandra Vidyasagar and, towards his lasting years, the brilliant Narendra Nath Dutt. Ramakrishna died on 16 August 1886 leaving behind a group of trained disciples—the onus of formally organising them into a monastic order devolved upon Narendra, soon to take the title Swami Vivekananda. On 1 May 1897 after his America sojourn, he founded the Mission to promote the study of Vedanta; study and research in the arts, sciences, technologies; to train teachers in all branches of knowledge; to carry out mass educational work; and to establish, maintain, carry on and assist schools, colleges and universities. The order he set up has been housed since January 1899 in Belur, on the western bank of the Ganga.

Management and organisation
The Belur Math, the headquarters of the Ramakrishna order, was given legal status through a deed of trust in 1901. To systematise

its work, a society was registered in 1909 and its management vested in a governing body consisting of trustees—10 permanent members, the others elected every two years. Since the Mission's administration is mostly in the hands of monks of the Math, despite the two being distinct legal entities with separate branches and separate accounts, they are closely related. Both are headquartered at Belur, both do charitable and philanthropic activities, though the Math's emphasis is on religion. A number of their local branches are self-sufficient and generate their own funds. In most cases, adherents organise themselves as local units and then approach Belur for affiliation, which is granted after careful scrutiny. All followers of Ramakrishna, lay or monastic, may be members of the Ramakrishna Association, if elected at a meeting of the Association or nominated by the governing body. Many followers accept diksha or are initiated into the Mission for closer association.

The Mission and Math attract funds on the basis of the extent and nature of their work. Donations are made to specific areas of work like education, medical work, rural development and relief work. Both receive grants from the central and state governments and public bodies. They also receive free services from professionals like lawyers, doctors and engineers. The Bengali middle-class forms a pool of enthusiastic support. The faith of donors too is such that they are confident of the maximum utilisation of their contribution. Immovable property forms a major part of their assets as many a follower or associate bequeath houses and land to the Mission. The majority desire that funds be used for charitable work rather than worship or ritual. Donations are exempted from income tax under section 80G of the IT Act.

The Math and Mission serve the public in general, irrespective of caste, creed or nationality. Prominent among these are hospitals at Kolkata, Itanagar, Kankhal, Lucknow, Ranchi, Thiruvananthapuram, Varanasi and Vrindavan. Besides in-patients and out-patients, mobile dispensaries cater to patients in rural and tribal areas. As part of medical education, it runs many nurses training centres. Research in various branches of medical science, as also post-graduate degree and diploma courses, are conducted at the Seva Pratishthan, Kolkata. The Ranchi sanatorium and a clinic at New Delhi treat tuberculosis cases, while Seva Pratishthan and the Thiruvananthapuram hospital also do maternity and child welfare work.

This work has come to occupy a key place in the Mission's scheme of services. The limited funds and workers are allocated to centres located in rural and tribal areas, urban centres that take up rural development projects, and to educational and medical institutions in urban areas where rural people form a significant percentage of the beneficiaries. No direct financial aid is given to an NGO but they are provided with support and advice and, at times, allowed the use of Mission infrastructure to reach out to rural people. The Mission and Math spent ₹6.83 crore in this area in 1999-2000 besides the expenditure incurred by educational and medical institutions located in rural and tribal areas.

This is a major thrust area for the Mission. A total expenditure of about ₹1.5 crore was incurred in 1999-2000 and is now about ₹30 crore on relief and emergency work carried out in flood, cyclone and earthquake-affected areas. Besides, relief articles worth ₹37.65 lakh were distributed among the afflicted people. Cyclone shelters and house-cum-schools were built at many places. Rural development programmes were undertaken through activities like spill check dam, crop development, wastewater management, and orchard plantation.

Spiritual work and preaching

Both the Math and Mission lay stress on disseminating India's spiritual and cultural ideals and seeking to give shape to the Ramakrishna philosophy of the unity of religions. Their various centres establish real points of contact among people of different faiths with public celebrations, meetings, classes, publications, among other activities. In total, 210 libraries are maintained and at least 10 centres publish books on religion and 19 journals in many languages. Daily worship, religious classes and lectures are held at all centres engaged in educational, medical or general service. The Mission's secular nature is self-evident. Christmas and the birthdays of Muslim saints are observed, just as Durga Puja and Kali Puja, with prayers and rituals thereby reflecting the secular credentials.

II. The Chinmaya Mission

A rain-drenched Sunday morning. About 50 children, faces vivid and bright, practice Gita chanting in Sidhbari, a hilly suburb of Dharamshala town in the foothills of the Dhauladhar mountains in Himachal Pradesh. In another room, a group of women busy themselves on their sewing machines. Satya is just back from a session with lawyers in Dharamshala regarding the divorce proceedings of the pradhan's daughter; Jyoti, a trained physiotherapist, attends to handicapped children. Amidst all this, Sandeep prepares for a workshop with local pradhans on micro-planning and decentralisation in Kangra. In Delhi, Anita is organising a series of lectures on appreciation of Indian culture while Parveen discusses the intricacies of Vedanta with a study group. In Ernakulam, Kerala researchers are busy on reader-friendly monographs on philosophy. In the same state, at a Harihar school in Kannur, children of poor farmers are being taught carpentry and book binding. In Cuddapah, Andhra Pradesh, locals are working on wells, roads and irrigation facilities. In Houston, USA children are being taught bhajans and Puranic stories.

Myriad efforts, touching myriad lives, all inspired by just one man—Swami Chinmayananda. His mission, from the outset, was to motivate people to begin thinking and acting in a new and deeply responsible way so as to revitalise the society of which they were a part. The Mission states that its aim is "to provide to individuals from any background the wisdom of Vedanta and practical means for spiritual growth and happiness". The guru left his body on 3 August 1993 but his legacy lives in a vast, many-faceted organisation whose work straddles spiritualism and social work.

Sharkskin suits to ochre robes

So who was Chinmayananda? What inspired his mission? What prompted his metamorphosis from homespun khadi to British sharkskin suits and soon after to ochre robes? Like Adi Shankara a flattering analogy seems to have inspired this latter-day sage—he was born in Kerala, travelled to the Himalayas as a seeker of knowledge, and traversed the length and breadth of India to propagate the Vedanta. Only that he spoke in English, primarily addressing the Anglicised elite to which he belonged. Born Balakrishnan (8 May 1917) to an affluent family in Ernakulam—his father Kuttan Menon was a judge and nephew of the Cochin maharaja—he studied law and literature in Madras and Lucknow, albeit indifferently. He was drawn into the freedom movement, went to jail, briefly worked for a British Intelligence Communication Centre, and then joined the *Free Press Journal* in Bombay and later *National Herald* in Delhi as a journalist. But the engaging wit of local club evenings had begun an intense study of philosophy that filled his mind with doubt and questions. In 1947, he headed for the Himalayas as a skeptic but had in two years turned a renunciate monk. On 25 February 1949 his guru Sivananda gave Balakrishnan the name Chinmayananda, "the one who revels in the bliss which is pure consciousness."

The Gangotri plan

Three years were spent studying the Vedas with Swami Tapovanam, the greatest Vedic scholar of the time, and crisscrossing India, living in ashrams and sleeping under trees. What he saw left him "miserably disillusioned and disappointed about ... the stuff being doled out in the name of Hinduism" and he decided the time had come to take the knowledge of the Vedanta to the masses to "convert Hindus to Hinduism". The inspiration, in his own words, came as he sat on the banks of the Ganga. He embarked on what he would call the Gangotri Plan. In the plains, using the age-old metaphor of yajna, where ignorance is burnt in the purifying fire, the young swami started to unfold the secrets of Vedanta to all those who came to him, regardless of caste, creed or community. A highly unorthodox approach, since these had until then been considered an elite preserve. At the first yajna, in Pune in December 1951, only 18 people were present but it had the orthodoxy up in arms. Many even petitioned the Shankaracharya of Kanchi to stop him but the seer instead advised the Brahmins to go and listen to him. Thereafter, in his lifetime, he is said to have conducted no less than 576 yajnas.

As they increased in frequency, so did the crowds "for they soon realised he was talking about them and their daily struggles ... not the mouldy relics of an irrelevant tradition." Over the next

42 years, lakhs were inspired by his insight, oratory and wit. With the Vedanta as his base and a format that was neither aggressive nor fundamentalist but nevertheless Hindu, he inspired and motivated people. He happened at a time when India's moral fibre was under stress after long years of alien rule and people were eager to reconnect with religious roots. By 1953, his followers decided to form the Mission to give structure to the many activities flowing from him. (It is said when they informed him, he protested at first, "Don't start an organisation in my name, I have not come to be institutionalised.")

Within two years, Chennai alone had six centres, each with a library and programmes of Gita chanting and group discussions and soon others were mushrooming elsewhere. Some members started small clinics and schools for the poor—though it was only in 1964 that he voiced a suggestion that the Mission enter organised philanthropy. Today, it has over 240 centres around the world engaged in activities that include schools, colleges, hospitals, old age homes and rural development projects. Two initiatives that were particularly close to Swami Chinmayananda's heart are the Chinmaya Tapovan Trust (CTT) in Sidhbari and the work done in the field of education.

Vedanta in action

Kangra valley is one of those places that would sound a lot less picturesque if you factor in the endemic unemployment, the shortage of water and fuel, the lack of schools and the scarcity of public health. The CTT, set up in 1981 by the Swami to bring the fruits of progress to this corner of India, has wrought some positive changes. For example, there are balwadis to take care of the children while parents work, healthcare personnel are not that rare, and locals are finding opportunities to use their skills and earn a living. Some have experienced life-transforming changes. Kaushalya, 46, used to eke out a meagre income knitting and working in the fields. CTT wanted someone to help in the Chinmaya dispensary and Kaushalya, who had studied up to class IX, took on the job.

Today, she is a trained health guide and social animator and one of the pillars of CTT's Integrated Participatory Development Programme (IPDP). Her family too has prospered despite an alcoholic husband; her six children are all well settled. Take Santosh Chauhan, 34, from the remote village Jhyol, who was beside herself with despair having to deal with a disabled child and abject poverty. In 1992, she learnt tailoring at CTT in Sidhbari and started work from home as a seamstress. She has also started taking classes for local girls and by her own reckoning earns about ₹3,700 a month. At another level, there is Dr Kshema Metre or 'Doctor Didi', a paediatrician from Delhi's Maulana Azad Medical College and a staunch disciple of the Swami. After attending a camp in Sidhbari, she decided to start a primary healthcare project in six villages. Over the years, it evolved into the showcase IPDP that provides a range of services to about 370 villages in the district. One estimate is that it touches 30,000 people directly and over 15,00,000 indirectly. So successful is the programme that the National Bank for Agriculture and Rural Development (NABARD) in 1998 declared CTT a mother NGO and asked it to train people and replicate the programme in four northern states.

What is notable is the meagre financial inputs they function with. Over six years, the bulk (almost 61 per cent) has come from the Canadian International Development Aid (CIDA) which matches every dollar the Mission raises with two Canadian dollars. A typical year's figure is ₹70 lakh, about 40 per cent of which goes towards honoraria, transport and administrative expenses and approximately eight per cent for salaries. The rest is for infrastructure, maintenance, equipment, etc. Similarly, since 1992, Norwegian aid agency NORAD has been supporting the Chinmaya Sewa Centre with a grant of ₹40 lakh which goes towards purchase of looms, sewing machines, raw material and salaries of trainers. According to a study, 30 to 40 per cent of those who trained at the centre earn ₹1,000 to ₹1,500 a month from tailoring. NABARD also provides funding, contingent on the programme. Donors have changed over the years. From 1985-1990 it was USAID, 1990-93 it was Ford Foundation.

Voices and choices

The manner in which IPDP evolved is worthy of study. In the early years, as Dr Kshema Metre explains, work was restricted to outpatient care. But the women who came also spoke "of matters other than health. Of poverty, illiteracy, alcohol abuse and desertion by husbands". It was then that CTT decided to address self-participatory programmes to get the women to take the initiative, analyse their problems and look for solutions with help from the Mission and the state outreach services. The concept of mahila mandals was born in 1987; today there are over 270 mandals where women help each other. Also, once the concept of balwadis for the children of working mothers was there, courtesy one woman's idea, it caught on. Scores of balwadis have opened in the district, each with a trained teacher and an attendant. Every month, they report to CTT for refresher courses.

In 1994, the existing primary healthcare facilities were extended to include a Disability and Community Rehabilitation Programme, the first of its kind in the state. Today over 1,000 mentally and physically challenged children from 75 villages come to the centre for treatment and therapy otherwise available only in Shimla and Chandigarh. Other interventions include afforestation programmes and cleanliness and sanitation drives. In 1990, Sahyogini was introduced as an integrated programme to familiarise women with public office systems. In Legal Aid Cell, grassroots workers are trained to counsel women who have been deserted, deprived of their share of property or are in any other way discriminated against. They go to the courts, interact with lawyers and the judiciary, secure legal advice and aid for those who need it and even arbitrate among feuding parties. Divorce and desertion are near-endemic in the region, so in 1992 the Swami set up the Chinmaya Sewa Centre (CSC) with support from the Norwegian Agency for Development Cooperation (NORAD) to provide training in tailoring. In 1996, the weaving section was started with 30 looms; in 1997, carpet making. On completing the course, women can purchase the loom or sewing machine for a small amount about five per cent of actual cost so as to enable them to set themselves up. Later, CSC helps them market their products. Besides, a great deal is being done to make people, especially women, aware and informed via adult literacy classes where education goes beyond reading and writing to include discussions on health, social, political and gender issues. A considerable effort is being made to work with whole villages via panchayats and gram sabhas with workshops, etc., on micro-planning and decentralisation of power. CTT workers motivate women to get involved in local government a beginning has been made with the first few panchayat members. Over the years, CTT has trained 9,000 grassroots workers often starting with specific training in health or literacy but quickly acquiring multifaceted talent.

Dr Kshema Metre attributes much of the success of CTT to the Swadhaya programme that runs "like a thread" through all other activity. The idea, she says, is not just on making people independent but on uplifting them spiritually. Bhajans are sung and the Gita chanted at the beginning of a class or programme and every Sunday there are discussions and lectures on spiritual matters. As Dr Metre says, "the best form of philanthropy ... is to help them to find the divinity in themselves."

Cornerstones of progress

The participatory spirit is embodied in the mahila mandals and self-help groups (SHGs). These address economic issues through micro-credit, micro-banks and income generation schemes that suit women's interests and resources; they also tackle social and health concerns. The mandals, for instance, have faced down the rampant alcohol abuse in the area—counselling men to give up drinking, staging dharnas against errant shops. Generally, an SHG has a dozen members who chip in ₹20 a month. These are banked and used to get loans with the group standing surety. Initially women hesitated to take an interest rate loan but one successful example always sets off a ripple effect. Over 12,000 women have availed of loans to start mushroom and orchid farming, to buy looms and sewing machines, etc. Participation in this programme has become more demand-driven, requiring less effort by CTT. Seeing the successes, banks which initially hesitated to get involved are "falling over each other in wanting to give loans". Today there are 908 SHGs in 370 villages in Kangra district and with each member putting in ₹20 it has resulted in a credit mobilisation of almost ₹4 crore among these poor women. Repayment is an impressive 100 per cent. If a member defaults, "the others go and find out why". The most important lesson from these successes is that programmes must be dynamic, flexible and process-oriented rather than target-oriented. Beneficiaries must progress from being passive receivers to become partners. Participation should be built into the system.

Education: seeds of spirituality

The Swami's emphasis on children as a vital target group and a symbol of renewal (Gita-chanting children would open his yajnas) saw the birth of Bal Vihars, where children were initiated into the basic vocabulary of Vedanta. In 1959, a children's section was added to the Mission to supervise the activities of the dozens of Bal Vihars that had sprung up. Today, there are thousands of adults who speak with gratitude of the benefits they reaped from associating with these Bal Vihars as children. The Chinmaya Yuva Kendra was formed to help those in the 16-28 age group actualise their potential and kindle latent abilities through the study of the scriptures. About 100 such groups exist today in India and abroad, organising and executing cultural, spiritual and social programmes.

This focus on the young turned Chinmayananda's attention to teachers and the whole pedagogical structure—and the many removes it stood vis-a-vis traditional ideals. At the first of many teachers' conferences (Bombay, 1960), he described education as the "transformation of knowledge into wisdom" and lamented India's adoption of the West's system where "facts and figures are stuffed into the child to be vomited out at exam time". His idea that self-actualisation is a prolonged process and the early inculcation of a spiritual core a vital component of this motivated a devotee to open a nursery school in Kollangad in 1965. Others followed in rapid succession, with the Mission laying down the basis of a secular, value-based system that incorporated key elements of Indian culture and civilisation.

Once the nursery schools stabilised, new classes were added every year. In time, high schools too came up. Today, there are 75,000 children enrolled in 71 Chinmaya Vidyalayas affiliated to the CBSE and state boards. There is also the Chinmaya International School in Coimbatore, affiliated to the CBSE and the Baccalaureate (Geneva), and two Harihar schools where poor students receive vocational training in addition to academics. Distinguishing them from the average school is the Chinmaya Vision Programme (CVP) that the Mission has developed to complement the academic programme. This aims at a child's integrated spiritual and intellectual development, offers a wide exposure to Indian culture, and instills civic consciousness as well as a universal outlook sensitive to world issues and the environment. The CVP is so successful that 500 schools not affiliated to the Mission have adapted it. At the university level, there are six colleges in Kerala, Karnataka, and Uttarakhand and the Mission has several more on the anvil. On the spiritual side, his dream to build "arsenals of rearmament" where youth willing to sacrifice personal concerns for a life of service could get rigorous training in Vedanta bore fruit when in 1963 the first Sandeepany Sadanalaya was opened with a five-year course. Now there are five of them, with a reduced course span, besides over 1,000 study groups, a beginner's correspondence course, a three-month residential course and dozens of weeklong camps that have made Vedanta accessible to the laity.

The organisation

From a one-man campaign to take Vedanta to the masses, the Chinmaya Mission has evolved in 50 years into a developmental organisation with 280 centres spread the world over. This runs on a loose federal structure of near-autonomous zonal centres manned to a great extent by the laity, because the swamis and swaminis are but 250. At the apex stands the Central Chinmaya Mission Trust (CCMT), formed in July 1964 and headquartered in Mumbai. Headed by Swami Tejomayananda, it comprises a CEO (the administrative head) and a dozen trustees. This body takes all major policy decisions and coordinates the activities of institutions under it. This includes seven zonal centres, each headed by a swami appointed for three to five years, with a board of 10-12 trustees. The latter in turn take on volunteers, a key link because, unlike some other religious bodies, the Chinmaya Mission is not about membership strength. In all there are 30,000 paid members the world over, though innumerable more partake of the activities.

Because of this federal structure, an overall assessment is difficult as no annual general body meeting is held or annual report prepared. Every two months, the zonal trustees meet and the minutes are sent to the headquarters new projects are started after approval. The Mission is registered as a charitable trust "with the main objective of promoting and spreading Indian culture and education among the masses". This way, it avails of tax benefits not available to religious bodies. Even funding is totally decentralised, though CCMT does help out with major projects and in times of emergencies. The bulk of funds come from donations, guru dakshina given to pracharaks after a yajna, fundraising drives and sale of books and cassettes.

III. Tirumala Tirupati Devasthanams

In the Eastern Ghats of Chittoor district, Andhra Pradesh, there is a cluster of hills with seven principal peaks, the Edukondalu. Here, the township of Tirumala houses the temple of Sri Venkateswara, one of India's foremost Vaishnava centres and the site of spiritual and cultural integration for pilgrims from all sections and regions of India. Its significance as one of the oldest religious sites in the world, with worship carried on continuously for 1,300 years has seen the number of pilgrims increase from 35,000 a day in 1984 to 60,000, often touching a lakh. At the foot of these hills, 22 km away, is Tirupati. The temples of Govindarajaswamy here and Goddess Padmavati at Tiruchanoor, 4 km away, complete the sacred triangle. The Tirumala Tirupati Devasthanams (TTD) undertakes their joint administration and circulates the giant corpus of money in a range of educational and philanthropic activity. The actual date of the construction of the temple is not clear—although the earliest mention seems to be in Tolkappiam, a second century BC work. The temple seems to have taken seven recorded stages to reach the final form, beginning from a standing murthi in an open mandapa from at least the first or second century AD, to the construction of a small garbha griha and ardha mandapa during the Pallav period (9th-10th century), extensive renovation during the thirteenth century AD under the Pandyan kings, up to the modem shrine following the Vijayanagar architectural style. During this last period, the temple acquired unprecedented glory. The epigraphs of Hampi give us extensive details regarding the nature of its administration and income. Today, no other temple attracts so many devotees or is as opulent. The following table traces the growth in recent decades.

History of management

The proper and efficient management of the temple was aided greatly by the degree of autonomy it received at all times. A long line of Hindu kings donated copious funds for construction and expansion, whereas the Muslim rulers and the British recognised its significance and scrupulously refrained from interference. The East India Company introduced a definite set of rules, contained in the Bruce Code of 1821, systematising practices and including the tahsildar in the management. In 1841, the directors of the Company chose to withdraw totally from management and passed it on to the head of the Hathiramji Math in Tirupati. This inaugurated an era that saw mahants as trustees—setting off much mutual acrimony and civil and criminal cases. Finally, this inauspicious period closed with the Madras State taking over in 1933, an onus that later passed to Andhra Pradesh.

The new state enacted a separate act in 1979 to streamline governance. The TTD was given charge of maintaining 10 temples. According to the Principal Act 30 of 1987, the state government would every three years constitute a trust board called the Tirumala Tirupati Devasthanams Board comprising not more than 13 members, including a state appointed chair, three MLAs, one scheduled caste member and one woman. A TTD management committee too was allowed for, with a stipulated membership pattern. The Act specified the pattern of budget approval and fund utilisation too. The TTD would have to deposit funds in the notified bank or securities. It is also common for the government to channelise TTD funds into public projects, such as the super-speciality Sri Venkateswara Institute of Medical Sciences, the Tirupati underground drainage project and the Telugu Ganga Water Supply Scheme.

Revenue

As its popularity grew, so did the inflow of money. Annual income, ₹2-3 lakh in 1908, increased to ₹50 crore in 1984, ₹380 crore in 2001 and nearly ₹500 crore in 2001-2002. In conclusion, the pilgrims in direct interviews expressed general satisfaction at the facilities provided at Tirumala, although quite a few spoke of the average devotee's difficulty in obtaining accommodation and getting darsanam. Some TTD staff also felt more investment needs to be made towards creating facilities to pilgrims. Major individual donors too wanted better treatment. Members from important NGOs thought there is far more scope—in terms of the depth of resources the TTD enjoys for it to earmark funds for NGO programmes. This way, TTD welfare efforts could be sharpened. As a conduit of public resources, it could thus play a more meaningful role while enhancing its image.

IV. Jnana Prabodhini

Psychologist Appasaheb Vinayak Vishwanath Pendse was initially a Rastriya Swayamsevak Sangh (RSS) pracharak. However, if that implies a certain shared conceptual template on issues like nationalism and commitment to a Hindu' ethos, there was a crucial gap in the degree of liberal-humanist spirit within which this could be realised. Dr Pendse left the RSS in 1952 and, a decade later, founded the Jnana Prabodhini (later renamed, henceforth JP) in Pune, Maharastra. This was visualised as a movement—with education at its core—that aimed to develop leadership in all non-political walks of life, so as to create conditions for social change. It targeted primarily the Maharashtrian community, and was built around a few core truths. Most importantly, that there exists no conflict between spiritualism and science, and both could be combined and oriented to the ultimate aim of building the nation at its human level. Although this was grounded in broad Hindu spiritualism, JP takes its non-denominational aspect seriously and is open to all. A paper by Girish Bapat cited "psycho-diversity" to validate a plural, personal realisation of the "one" ideal.

Prashala, a school with Marathi as the medium of instruction, is the mother institution on which the foundation of the whole organisation rests. It was started in 1969 with loans from banks and private individuals. When the financial burden proved too heavy to be sustained for long, JP started exploring alternative ways to generate resources. The solution was found in an integrative model, where one tier of activity feeds the other. In 1971, the Kirloskar Foundation helped set up a 50-lathe factory at Shivaganga. Now JP's industrial activity has swollen to three units, one engaged in publishing literature from the National Council of Educational Research and Training, University Grants Commission, Council for Advancement of People's Action and Rural Technology and the District Rural Development Agencies, one in manufacturing elevators and the third capacitors. This helped blend rural development, industrial training and building of entrepreneurship. Prashala students sell articles from JP's own rural development projects, raising funds for both the school and the project itself. Around Diwali, they buy products like crackers, et al, at wholesale prices and retail to the community. This not only helps in fund generation, it trains students in real financial activity. Public donations also form a vital component—usually from ex-students and alumni who give guru dakshina to the mother institution. There is a 1,000-student database from the 1960s till the present, a pool that cherishes its involvement with the alma mater. Prabod, a group founded in 1988 by entrepreneurs who believe in a ceiling on individual income, dedicates a percentage of profits from their consulting, human resource development and software companies to Jnana Prabodhini. Many work for a low honorarium for the institution and its programmes. The teachers, many with doctorates, too willingly work at low salaries. In a way, it is a dedicated fraternity with strong organisational ethic built around simplicity.

There is recognition that such an approach may also stunt growth. Jnana Prabodhini's answer is that maybe only one in 20 persons are cut out for positions of leadership in the way JP defines it working to give back to society. JP sees its task as being able to collect together a nucleus of 10 to 12 people, for instance, dedicated doctors from among the pool of alumni who can coordinate with a hundred other doctors to maintain standards. This is how the Janna Prabodhini Medical Trust was set up in 1993, with a team of young doctors taking over the Sanjeevani hospital in Pune. Such leadership needs to be ascetic in lifestyle, perhaps a hard ideal in this day and age. But JP steadfastly works towards this ideal, partnering NGOs, corporates, trusts, even the government, to expand its reach to every district in Maharashtra.

In its rural thrust, it is also involved in projects to do with watershed development, biogas and other renewable resources. JP conducts vocational training, entrepreneurship development programmes and disseminates improved agriculture practices. In health, a major record has been its success in reducing the incidence of leprosy from 5 to 0.37 per thousand in a population of 2.25 lakh. Overall, its website lists:

- Eight educational institutions, including schools in Pune, Solapur, Nigdi, and Salumbre;
- Six rural development programmes;
- Three research institutes engaged in Ayurveda, Psychology and Sanskrit and Indology;
- Six industrial and apprenticeship units;
- Sanjeevani Hospital in Pune;

- Eye hospital in Shirwal;
- A comprehensive rural scheme in Shivapur.

The Prashala

The Prashala is situated in Sadashiv Peth, the he art of Pune's Brahmin orthodoxy and culture. Dr Pendse, whose thesis on leadership styles is the core of its philosophy, modelled it as an institution that could develop a generation of leaders in all walks of life. The school selects its students through tough testing, involving intelligence models, in the conviction that training the gifted from an early age is the way to evolve leadership. Education is highly subsidised in 1979, the school spent ₹2,000 a year per student and charged only ₹200. Study tours are taken to be a vital part of the learning process here, supplementing textbook inputs in geography, history and politics. The school stresses experiential understanding over mere theory. For example, students visited Punjab just before Operation Bluestar in 1984 and interviewed journalists, administrators, figures like Sant Longowal and even the militant guru Bhindranwale. After the Sati at Deorala, girl students visited the village and tried to understand the popular psyche that allowed such an incident. The girls, from a progressive part of Maharashtra, had a shocking but revelatory introduction to the position of women in a backward state. A group of students recently travelled across Kashmir to know the feelings of locals. They visited many locations, interviewed a large cross-section of people and came back with revelations not commonly reported by the media.

Psychology and Indology

The Department of Psychological Research and Testing, established around 1976, evolves and carries out research projects in educational psychology, social psychology, industrial psychology and also yogic psychology. Thus, it provides a theoretical matrix for the actual core of JP's activities. The notion of leadership and giftedness derives from this area and the process of testing students for intelligence before admission to Prashala can be linked to the fact that Mensa, the international group for high IQ and intelligence testing, has its India office at Jnana Prabodhini.

Santrika, denoting Sanskrit-Sanskriti-Sanshodhika, is firstly a storehouse of books in Sanskrit and, next, a postgraduate and doctoral research institution to conduct traditional scholarship in Indology and also to study questions like the synthesis of yoga and knowledge. This bases itself on the view of Sanskrit as an ancient language that has hosted and promoted rational inquiry along many axes to form Adhyatma Vidya, the science of man in depth. It also undertakes fundamental and applied research in culture, language and literature. It also aims to reinterpret and make available the contribution of the 16 sanskaras in Sanatana Dharma through the publication of booklets, texts and modem audiovisual tools.

Industry

The mechanical division was started with machines donated by industrial houses. In March 1971, 50 lathe machines were donated by the Kirloskars, and job work was given by them. The Shivaganga valley project was started with donated machines worth ₹25 lakh. They produced components for Kirloskar Oil, Engines, Telco and Bajaj Auto. The fabrication division makes hand pumps, gobar gas plants, cranes and milk cans. Prabodhan Capacitors, set up with initial capital and raw materials donated by the French Committee for Universal Campaign Against Hunger, started selling orders worth over a crore to state electricity boards in Gujarat, Haryana, Maharashtra and Tamil Nadu since 1975-78. The Khandsari sugar manufacturing division was started at Gunjavani river valley with help from Christian Aid, Boston. Jnana Prabodhini students learn management and engineering skills at all these units.

Rural health

Jnana Prabodhini's comprehensive rural health programme covers 236 villages and a total population of over two lakh spread over 1,050 sq km in Shivaganga and Gunjawani valleys. A leprosy eradication programme has been running here since 1982, supported by Swiss NGO Emmaus. Also running are a basic health programme in Velhe taluka, multipurpose clinics in remote villages, a full-fledged eye hospital at Shirval, an out-patient department (OPD) at Shivapur, periodic check-up, awareness and surgery camps, rehabilitation programmes for cured leprosy patients, and promotion of naturopathy, yoga and ayurvedic treatments.

The Nirmay hospital, started in 1999 by the Dabhol Power Charitable Trust, has a contract with Jnana Prabodhini, which is entrusted with running the 50-bed hospital with five general practitioners, a surgeon, a gynaecologist and an OPD. Similarly, the Lata Mangeshkar Medical Foundation-promoted Master Dinanath Mangeshkar hospital, a ₹25 crore, 450-bed ultramodern affair with 12 operation theatres, nurses' training school and kidney transplant centre has tied up with the Jnana Prabodhini Medical Trust, with its reputation for providing quality medical care at reasonable cost.

The branches

The Jnana Prabodhini, Solapur chapter, is active in two districts, covering a population of 8,06,000 and working in agriculture, education, forestry, health and sanitation, rural entrepreneurship, slum development, etc. It relies on donations from friends and well-wishers for its capital expenditure.

The Shivapur chapter has a training-cum-production institute, set up in 1971, where over 2,000 rural youth have been trained until now. An amount of ₹1 crore has been distributed and invested through its activities. An agro-technical workshop was begun in 1981 and a farmers' cooperative for managing water distribution, dams and biogas development followed. The Gram Prabodhini Vidyalaya at Salumbre village, in collaboration with the Rotary Club of Pune (North), is an attempt to make education in the rural areas relevant and contextual so it does not uproot students from the rural community but facilitates their efforts to pioneer change. The education offered here encompasses agriculture, vocational guidance, forestry, animal husbandry, etc., and seeks to blend formal and informal education.

The school at Nigdi, similarly, attempts to create a community-based centre for development touching educational, cultural, social, health and spiritual aspects and replicate and validate a variety of experiments conducted at Prashala in a different sociocultural environment, an industrialised suburb.

Conclusion

Jnana Prabodhini, thus, is a unique institutional-building process that aims to cultivate a Hindu intellectual, spiritual and entrepreneurial renaissance. It encourages entrepreneurship and self-help, instead of targeting "outsiders" as done by the Shiv Sena. It creates socially relevant health and development programmes and encourages the spirit of inquiry.

It has created an immense pool of supporters from individuals, corporates, academics, family trusts, funders and professionals. It is unique in its blend of science and spirituality, industry and rationalisation of rituals (like having thread ceremony for girls). This is based "on a realisation that Western modernity in toto and the cut-and-dried secularism of the academic 'hands off' variety will not work in India. It would be difficult to match the JP board in terms of scientists, social activists and responsible corporate citizens—inter alia, former Socialist Party chairman SM Joshi, prominent industrialist SL Kirloskar, Anna Hazare, Dr Jayant Narlikar, Raja Ramanna and Dr Mashelkar (all scientists).

ISLAMIC PHILANTHROPY

Any attempt to map this territory will have to confront an entrenched conceptual problem. In a modern universal discourse (such as the one this document inhabits), this can be described as a problem related to producing knowledge of Islam or its adherents. The first danger here is from a kind of self-perpetuating dogma. The West's sophisticated empiricism and the Islamic scholar's inside account, both are equally culpable of lapsing into this curiously powerful metaphor at one level of imagination. Consequently, analyses derive from, and in turn feed, one basic proposition: that Islam is a homogeneous entity and Muslims, irrespective of cultural, social and political contexts, share an inevitable bond of community. This presumed homogeneity, if located politically, represents a totalising, closed and fundamentalist image, justifying the popular notion that Islam is an antithesis to democracy or popular participation. The marked polarity that has emerged in global affairs after 11 September 2001 has made these tendencies more keenly felt. For our purpose, it renders all the more urgent the task of injecting a larger dose of rationalism and historical awareness into analysing Islamic philanthropy, so that its sundry strands and shades in India can be situated with more authenticity in their own specific contexts—ideological, political and social-historical.

The above prelude was necessary in the wake of the global war against terrorism, which, for all the demurrals, is implicitly seen by all parties concerned to have chosen a vaguely defined Islamism as its target. And in doing so, it has further imposed a fuzzy unity on all forms of Islamic social and political organisation. In India, the ban on the fringe group Students Islamic Movement of India (SIMI) exacerbated an illiberal climate where the credibility of all Muslim social or political groupings is being interrogated. Even nationalist organisations such as the Jamiat-Ulema-e-Hind and Darul-Uloom Deoband, which played a significant role in the freedom struggle, are being subjected to this tremendous pressure. This either/or, totalising approach is apt to deflect attention from the genuine issues of the marginalised sections among Muslims, who are doubly distressed. Within the community, the elite is reluctant to introspect on or discuss the internal contradictions, while the surcharged atmosphere outside is forcing the common Muslim to search for identity within the ambit of the same totalising project of the Muslim elite. Philanthropic organisations have to constantly face threats from the state even while doing good.

This is the context in which we study philanthropic activities, whose manifestations are in any case vast and complex. Beneath a commitment to the supremacy of Allah, the one God, the Quranic scripture, faith in the prophethood of Mohammad and a conception of a universal community that can be found everywhere, the cultural and regional configurations of Islam viz. the local practices, dialects of modernity and the structural dynamics of power overlap at every level of Indian society. This hybridisation of Muslim identity is peculiar and unique. Islam provides bedrock to these varied forms but the interpretations of texts, and the ways and degree to which religious authority is enmeshed with social hierarchies and power structures can show remarkable variation. India, too, is conceived as a special and distinct geocultural reality. Its physical distance from the centres of Islam not only determines this cultural remoteness from the dominant 'ultimate Islam' but also makes provision for a regionalised Islamic socio-political discourse. The existence of the other is recognised, not as a mandatory form of Islamic identity, but as a dominant ramification of the Islamic world.

The philanthropic organisations that emerge from within such a plurality depend on flexible and contingent variables. These include the localised social hierarchies (caste, the biradari system); the ways in which Islam as an ideology was allowed to be assimilated and quite often resisted; the political-economic power graph that influences this hybrid identity and its representation; and the ways in which modernist Islam cohabits with these. There are broad differences on this within scholarship. One position is that there are two Islams in India—the first is ultimate and formal, derived from texts such as the Quran and Hadith; the second proximate and local, validated by custom, and crucial in determining an Islamic political identity in India. Another sees a tendency among Indian Muslims to survive for an ultimate and ideal Muslim life. Yet another privileges the day-to-day life struggles of Muslims as the vantage point over and above any Islamic content. This affords us a rich socio-political backdrop in which to locate Islamic philanthropy, we shall veer towards the first thesis and also look at grassroots struggles against a matrix of class, caste and gender.

The growth of the voluntary sector in India has seen a departure from state-run, bureaucratic programmes. The typical Third World cycle of debt has compelled the state to roll back populist schemes, ceding to civil society organisations. This presents a chance to shift to a people-oriented approach of development. Experience has shown that imposed knowledge could not adequately address concerned groups and only a section of the society got the benefits of state welfarism. The cultural and social gap between policy and people created a situation where an imperialism of categories prevailed. In this respect, civil society organisations may do well to respect religious philanthropy for its rooted categories and concepts, for the different kind of access they provide to the community and to sustain the possibility of linking up meaningfully with this sector.

In contemporary India, the Muslim community is characterised as a crisis-ridden one. The state, social sector, the civil society common to Muslims all share this thesis and propose different solutions. Maybe all marginalised communities (and organisations working with them) mobilise internal resources and external support by emphasising the uneven position of its members. Yet, the Muslim case is unique insofar as the crisis is not only social but also somehow to do with religion, fixed Islam, thus, mediates even developmental activities. There is a lot of misunderstanding that there is no civil society in Islam. I have tried to remove this misconception.

The concept of charity in Islam

The conceptual territory occupied here—if one means to denote by the term Islamic philanthropy a set of benevolent activities aimed at giving material support to the downtrodden within and outside the community, in the name of Allah—is such that it takes in simple material charity and concerted social action. But this overarching concept has scriptural bases from which it cannot deviate. The most frequently recurring word for charity in the Quran is Infaq (spending benevolently). This has three necessary, related assumptions: (a) charity has to be from halal (lawful) earned income; (b) all wealth belongs to Allah, thus the individual only decides how much they return to the real owner; and (c) there are two forms of charity—one obligatory, the other voluntary. This last helps tie the concept of charity to other forms of prescribed religious acts in Islam—the five essential tenets of Tauheed, Salat, Zakat, Roza and Haj. Tauheed is a strong belief in Allah, the one God, and the Prophethood of Mohammed; Salat is the five daily prayers; Zakat means the purification of lawfully earned wealth through proper and prescribed distribution; Roza is fasting; and Haj means pilgrimage. In all these, a spiritual individual aspect is bound with social action. No one can perform devout acts without the community—social action can be seen to be an inseparable part of Islam.

The notion of charity as the act of an individual, who spends wealth for personal satisfaction, is not applicable in Islam. It has a rather more engaged social sense. It is not merely the duty of an individual who has wealth but also the right of the poor to get their share. Wealth, as the Quran explains, does not belong to individuals. The Almighty is the real and absolute owner of all things the individual's position is somewhat equivalent to that of a trustee. The category of obligatory charity takes in Zakat. The other category, voluntary, includes Wakf, Fitrah, Sadqa, Hiba and, in the Indian context, Chadhawa (offerings). Zakat is the most important philanthropic act in Islam and literally means to purify, to develop or cause to grow. In fact, it is the third pillar of Islam. If a person entitled to pay Zakat is not paying their dues, they will not be considered a Muslim at all. The wealth of such a person is impure because of not fulfilling social obligations.

Zakat is not applicable to all Muslims. But every rich Muslim (Saheb-e-Mall), who possesses property equal to or exceeding a minimum exemption limit (Nisab), has to pay Zakat at the prescribed rate. The Nisab calculates movable and immovable property, cash, gold, silver, animals, agricultural products (ushar) and other items that are regarded as profitable sources of income. The recipients of Zakat include the following categories:

- Fuqara (Poor): Those whose possessions do not reach the minimum Nisab limits;
- Masakin (The needy): Those whose earnings are not enough to satisfy the essential need of themselves and their dependents;
- Amilun: Those engaged in the collection and distribution of Zakat through a community;
- Mu-allafatu-al Qulub: Those who need immediate rehabilitation;
- Riqab: For the ransom of captives, wherever such necessity arises;
- Garimum: Debtors;
- Ibn-as Sabil: The traveller who is not poor but is stranded abroad without funds;
- Fi Sabi-Lillah: Those engaged in religious work.

In countries where Islamic laws are promulgated, Zakat is centrally administered and collected as welfare tax. In other countries, various organisations perform this duty. In India, Zakat money is given individually. As a result, the institution of Zakat is not effectively addressing the needs of the community. The Zakat Foundation of India is now planning to take concrete steps in this direction.

Of the voluntary forms of Islamic philanthropy in India, Wakf is perhaps the central one, placed along with Fitrah (religious giving), Sadqa (derived from Sidq, truth) and Hiba (gifts). To these established acts of benevolence were added a new form—Chadhawa (offering) in medieval India as devotees at a dargah paid for langar (feast) and maintenance. This happened as Sufism produced a synthesis of local culture and the doctrine of Islam, out of which evolved new meanings of charity.

Wakf, literally, means detention or stoppage. According to the Hanafi School of Islamic law, it denotes the extinction of the proprietor's ownership in the thing dedicated and its detention in the implied ownership of God in such a manner that the profits may revert to and be applied for the benefit of human beings. So, theoretically, this has three interrelated components. First, the owner of the property; second, their dedication of that property in the name of Allah; and third, society as the beneficiary of that dedicated portion of property. Since God is not a material entity, the society and community which is the actual heir would exercise its control through the Muttawalli (the person appointed by the owner as a manager of Wakf property).

Interestingly, there is no direct mention of Wakf in the Quran the term being derived from the Hadith. Islamic jurists identify Quranic verses that indicate its possibility. These verses, along with the Hadith and a few well-known injunctions of Fiqh (Islamic jurisprudence), define the practical modalities of Wakf.

Wakf institutions in post-colonial India carry two important aspects. First, it is a minority institution where the state has the sole authority to legislate and supervise its functioning. In this sense, Wakf is akin to a government department. All state governments appoint a minister for Wakf issues. At the central level, it comes under the Ministry of Social Justice and Empowerment. Secondly, though it is the largest Islamic philanthropic institution in India, unlike other religious boards, Wakf is not controlled by the community. The state nominates people to these institutions, or they are elected by the Muslim elite. In this sense, the participatory principle for establishing transparency, effectiveness and democratic management is lost.

A historical sketch

In pre-British India, the lack of a universal image of community and the low communication level confined the scope of philanthropy to a local level, geographically, and conceptually to a ritualistic mode. Religion itself was understood in relative, cultural terms—so was the case with philanthropy. Historians identify two co-existing aspects of medieval religion—the dominant, ideal, textual, sacred and perfect ritualistic mode; and multiple manifestations of local beliefs. Local philanthropy was naturally more influenced by local belief systems. The ideal-type religion only provided an outline; its modus operandi was rooted in local culture and practices. For example, during the Sultanate period, the rulers themselves collected Zakat and Jaziya, but these forms of taxation were not properly universalised.

The colonial period marked a departure in the social history of India. India as a geocultural entity acquired a fixed territorial definition and experienced a universalised project of modernity. The British-initiated changes in the political arena were backed by modem education. The totality of colonial discourse was oriented to subordinate India by employing a variety of measures—economic, social and, in a way, cultural. Religion and history were vital ingredients in the specific system of knowledge the British evolved, which conceptualised India as a combination of competitive identities. The educational institutions produced the carriers of this rational, scientific, modern knowledge. As loyal upper middle class elite grew in various communities, the colonial notion of difference was absorbed.

Islamic philanthropy evolved in this context. Muslims had to face a peculiar pressure. The general backwardness of common Muslims, a direct result of British economic policies, was interpreted as the crisis of the community as a whole. The elite Muslim leadership overlooked the real economic and social issues, and often represented spontaneous subaltern resistance as communal conflict. Though this was in response to a climate where the Hindu reformists—ignoring historic Islamic contribution—had started to glamorise ancient India as the real India.

The tendency towards classical religion became dominant in this period. The codification of laws consolidated the perception that the ideal and sacred religion was the real religion. Local understanding, practices and rituals receded in importance. The process of enumeration on the basis of religion (in 1871, the first census data was released) helped the elite speak the language of a closed homogeneous community, minority-majority politics and protectionism.

Broadly, two kinds of social organisations emerged during this period. The first was highly localised, secular and relatively progressive. This included day-to-day philanthropic activities such as weekly charity (e.g., on Thursday), charity related to birth, marriage and death rituals, festivals and Chadhawa at dargahs. The second form was religiously orthodox and politically modern—the Darul-Uloom at Deoband and the Aligarh Muslim University offer two varied examples. The Deoband madrassa, which emerged during the nineteenth century, represented the anti-British character of Indian Islam. Although the madrassa did share the community-in-crisis thesis, it openly supported Indian nationalism and Hindu-Muslim unity. The anti-Western movement launched by Shah Waliullah and Sayed Jamal-ud-din Afghani provided a key impulse in this. Unfortunately, Deoband did not go further and only radicalised a closed form of Islam.

Syed Ahmed Khan best represented the modem Muslim elite who favoured a liberal-modernist philanthropy. These elite followed specific kind of politics. They accepted the modern vocabulary of minority and majority and condensed their political operation within the boundaries of their minority status. Such activities suited the British agenda and they offered encouragement, often with legislation. The Bengal Code 1810 and the Madras Code 1817, which provided power to the state to manage the affairs of religious endowments, were repealed to hand over the management of Muslim religious endowments to loyal Muslims. The various Wakf Acts and separate representation in legislatures further divided the people in the name of religion. Ultimately, in 1947, Pakistan came into existence.

After the transfer of power in 1947, the new Indian state took up the burden of modernity—reshaping India, survivor of the colonial project, along socialist tenets with a huge public sector. Islamic philanthropy too entered another phase. The state started supporting nationalist Islamic philanthropic activities. The nationalist-modernist elite who had joined the national freedom struggle with the Congress found a new status as the community leaders. Of course, the state could withdraw or transfer its support. This became evident in the 1970s when the nationalist Muslim elite joined the JP movement, and the Congress-led state encouraged the religious elite among Muslims. Imam Syed

Abdullah Bukhari is the best example of this sort of politics. Ayodhya engulfed public discourse at a time when the Indian state was preparing to roll back from its own established notion of welfarism. Communal politics only added to the common Muslim's economic hardship, cultural degradation and emotional insecurities. Unfortunately, the progressive-secular forces did not reach out to the common Muslim and only interacted with the self-claimed community leaders. It was left to a few large-scale Muslim organisations to interact with the people.

Contemporary philanthropy

We have already listed the six kinds of Muslim organisations now working in India. In the first instance, we can count small local madrassas and dargahs. Although this type of philanthropy places importance on ritual, its progressive content cannot be ignored. Notably, because local social issues often come within its ambit. Participation in local social movements like that of the landless labourers in Bihar's Jehanabad district also makes it relevant. Such organisations receive no outside support. As a result, the mainstream voluntary sector does not identify them. These organisations function at the bottom level of society, from where they also mobilise resources. After 11 September 2001, such bodies suffered a lot of pressure, especially in the border areas of western Rajasthan. The state targeted small madrassas for their alleged role in promoting fundamentalist Islamic education. The Gujarat riots too targeted this marginalised end of society. So little is understood of these organisations by the state that many are targeted by intelligence bureaus and also by right-wing militants.

Under primordial-modernist, we can club organisations that emerged out of the religious tradition. They can be said to have modified the traditional form of religious giving to some extent, harmonising it with modem management in order to channelise prescribed charity both for religious works and the community's social development. In north India, few mosques or shrines have ventured herein but Jammu's Dargah Shahdara Sharif is an illustration. In the south, they are more visible: for instance, the Bima Palji in Kerala. Such bodies receive donations and offerings. They also rely upon the huge number of visiting devotees, as also upon Zakat money.

Those organisations, established to do social work within the community with a fair bit of emphasis on Islamic culture and identity, can be put in the liberal-modernist category. Management of community resources is a key aim for them: they raise funds from the community towards social development projects. Notably, these organisations represent themselves as liberal and secular. Though they often commit to work exclusively for Muslims; being active in fields like education makes them accessible to the general public. This helps disseminate a liberal image of Islam. They raise money from the public, special collections from affluent Muslims, funds from non-resident Indian (NRI) Muslims (especially those in the Middle East), and state support. A few like Al-Ameen are self-sufficient: their own economic institutions provide them funds. In southern India, Zakat is a vital source of income for them. Financial aid from the Islamic Development Bank (IDB) often comes specifically for educational health. Cordial ties with Wakf institutions also helps most such organisations run institutions on Wakf land as does affiliation with universities and special support from state-run minority institutions.

Of the liberal-political type, the best examples are the Jamat-e-Islami and the Jamiat Ulema-Hind. These typically work as pressure groups, with the objective of protecting Islam through liberal-political means. With the base idea that Muslims in India not only represent Islam as a religion but also constitute a cultural minority, such organisations seek protection of minority rights. They believe in the empowering effect of education and also strive for legislative measures to achieve maximum space for Muslims. The three target groups of this type of philanthropy are the urban middle and lower classes and semi-urban land-owning classes. These kinds of organisations collect donations from cadres and also get funds from affluent Muslims and NRIs. Publication of Islamic literature too is a source of income for such groups, which propagate an orthodox liberal Islam, which is, to an extent, secular in nature.

Under state-run philanthropy fall the Wakf boards all over India, whose formation is based on Article 26 of the Constitution. Issues relating to Wakf figure at serial number 28 of the Concurrent List of the Seventh Schedule. In 1954, the first Wakf Act was passed, providing for the establishment of Wakf boards and delineating their functions, power and finances. It also provided for a survey, registration and the superintendence of all Wakf properties keeping the main objective of pious and religious purpose intact. A series of amendments (1959, 1964, 1969) led to a comprehensive amendment bill in 1984, based on the Wakf Inquiry Committee (1976) recommendations. But political factors scotched its enactment. A package of minority welfare schemes in 1991 paved the way for the Wakf Act 1995, which vested more control with the Board. The various boards—which engage in the field of education, organise Urs at dargahs, and dispense medical services—generate money from rent of Wakf properties and also receive bank loans and grants-in-aid.

Radical Islamism is a recent phenomenon, coming into

existence in the past 20 years in India. The polarisation of Hindu fundamentalism and the rise of pan-Islamism globally created the conditions for its growth. The Islamic texts, now clothed in radical interpretations, offer a prime tool to fundamentalists, whose key objective is to establish an Islamic state in this country. The influence of Arabic streams, which highlight radical components of Islam, is clearly present over this sort of organisation.

The state, law and Wakf

Wakf, unlike Zakat, is not obligatory philanthropy; it is, rather, a voluntary apportionment of property for community welfare. The fruits of Wakf are not limited to Muslims; they are a dedication to the benefit of all humanity (though Muslim law in India restricts Wakf primarily to Muslims). Now, Islamic charity favours close links between donor and beneficiary. The Quran advises all to identify the needy in family, biradari or khaandan (in a restricted sense, caste), locality or city. Thus, economic redistribution initiated at the level of family or immediate group is seen as means to secure substantive equality at all levels of society. But Wakf is significantly different from other forms of charity. It is a permanent dedication that produces long-term benefits in an invisible manner. This abstraction enhances its potential, embracing a larger number (Muslims and non-Muslims) within its fold.

The Fiqh lends to Wakf a transcendental sense. If a person dedicates a portion of property to the future, that portion transcends temporal boundaries. The person who creates the Wakf acquires the status of a waqif and transcends context. The Wakf too becomes a living monument, with the common right of people over it established by law. This does not by itself become a form of philanthropy unless the recipients of the flow of common good recognise it to be so. It devolves upon the Muttawalli to ensure the continuing utility of the Wakf and its just distribution. Wakf also symbolises a mode of affirming faith in Allah, whose authority is unique, ultimate and unquestionable. Islam forbids idolatry and, just like the Quran enables Allah's authority to be known, Wakf realises the ownership of Allah in material form.

Both the Act of 1954 and its colonial precursor, the Mussalman Wakf Validating Act 1913, define Wakf as a form of permanent "dedication, by a person (professing Islam), of any movable or immovable property for any purpose recognised by Muslim law as pious, religious or charitable". The theoretical accent here is clear. It falls on the individual who creates the Wakf, their objective, and modem Muslim law, which is authorised to define religious purposes. In short, modern codified law finds no place for the recipients in its analytical scheme of things.

The modes by which Shariat laws were adopted and codified as personal laws are another grey area. In the colonial attempts to trace the original roots of Muslim laws, the Quran, Hadith and other religious texts were taken as immutable sources of law. The wealth of written records was privileged over local customs and rituals that were deemed less pristine. These living traditions were described as the outcome of Hindu influence. More subtly, the community was not placed at the centre of the exercise. A legal system based on individualism was grafted on to community-oriented Islamic social practices. Individuals who professed a common religion replaced the notion of collective or group. The marginalisation of local shared values, with the extreme individuation of Islamic laws, curbed all scope of having a socially accepted, culturally accommodative Muslim Law.

In 1810, Regulation XIX of the Bengal Code was passed for

the due appropriation of rents and produce of lands granted to support mosques, temples and other religious endowments. A similar law was passed in 1817 in Madras. These regulations recognised the legal control of the colonial state over religious institutions (in the name of management) and brought local conflicts into this new public sphere. Such issues as had been solved at the local level without legal or political formalities were encoded in this new discourse, only to become endless symbols of conflict. Later, as an English-literate middle-class elite started claiming community leadership, such conflicts were consolidated in the overall construction of the past as communal history. The Wakf, which had lost its social character at that time, became another issue of contestation.

In 1840, British missionaries agitated against state involvement in managing non-Christian institutions. The events of 1857 also forced rethink on local practices and the extent to which the state could get involved. The Religious Endowment Act 1863 followed, ceding direct control to managers and managing committees with a proviso of intervention by the civil court. While fixing the state to an indirect, supervisory role, the Act also defined the boundaries of religious and charitable acts. Most crucially, it inserted a bifurcation between religious and secular domains by talking of endowments that were partly for religious purposes and partly secular—the Board of Revenue was empowered to decide which portion was which. The result was widespread confusion because it was unimaginable then to differentiate between pure Islamic charity and secular forms of charity.

There were also numerous practical anomalies, given its ambiguities on the rules, powers and functions of managers and committees and financial aspects. The state's legal control over a growing sector suffered from weak delineation. The Charitable and Religious Endowments Act 1920 sought to address these lacunae. Meanwhile, the ground situation altered significantly with the Government of India Act 1909 which made provisions for a separate electorate. This milestone in India's political history, which conceptualised legal separatism, was accompanied by interventions at a more practical level—with profound theoretical implications. One was the Wakf Validating Act 1913 that consolidated state control over Wakf institutions. Amidst a controversy over the state's legal meddling in established religious practices, the Act modernised the functioning of Wakf and brought the institution into a modern Muslim legal discourse in which there was no place for the community itself. The state was now the ultimate authority to interpret, translate and deliver justice on religious matters, an equation that passed unchanged from the colonial to the post-colonial situation.

Central Wakf Council

This agency was created under the Wakf Act 1954 to advise the government on matters relating to the functioning of Wakf boards and the proper administration of Wakf in India. The Act of 1995 reconstituted the council and it came into existence in its new form on 26 June 1997. The 20-member council has the union minister in charge of Wakf as the ex-officio chair and members nominated from among prominent Muslim organisations, parliamentarians, judicial figures, representatives of Wakf boards and Muttawallis, Islamic scholars and other eminences with administrative/financial expertise. All the Wakf boards in the country pay one per cent of their annual income as Wakf Fund to the council. The council looks after urban and rural Wakf properties and also runs educational schemes.

Since 1975, the government has been giving the council annual grants-in-aid for urban Wakf properties. This goes into loans to Wakf boards and institutions for (re)construction of commercially viable buildings on urban Wakf land. In 1997-98, the grant-in-aid was ₹1,586.11 lakh, of which ₹63.8 lakh was utilised to finance three projects in Rajasthan, Maharashtra and Kerala. In 1998, the council adopted an action plan to fund commercially viable rural properties up to ₹10 lakh. Till 15 January 2000, 60 of 84 projects initiated with grants-in-aid had been completed.

The council's education welfare schemes partly flow out of the former. It collects six per cent as donation on all loans related to urban Wakf properties. This is deposited as the education fund and goes to pay for:

- Scholarships to students pursuing technical and professional degree courses at ₹6,000 per year.
- Ad-hoc grant to poor and needy students of general degree course at ₹3,000 per annum.
- Matching grant to state Wakf boards for scholarship to students for diploma courses in technical education, higher secondary and madrassa education.
- 50 per cent matching grant to technical institutes to start fresh courses or strengthen existing trade courses.
- Financial assistance for vocational training.
- Financial assistance to book banks in school libraries.

Punjab Wakf Board

Constituted in October 1960, this is the only composite Wakf board in India. Since November 1981, it has been administered directly by the central government. It manages all Wakf properties in Punjab, Haryana and Chandigarh—the region where, after the partition of India, there remained a large number of abandoned Wakf properties, many of which went into illegal possession. The board has approximately 40,000 properties, many of them embroiled in litigation. The board also runs 10 schools, four computer centres and nine tailoring centres, besides assisting private organisations. In 1997-99, it offered financial assistance to 46 schools. In its basic area of activity, i.e., managing Wakf properties, the board gives money to many mosques, madrassas and dini maktabas, pays all the imams and muezzins, looks after the maintenance of mosques and madrassas and organises annual Urs at famous dargahs. It also provides financial assistance to destitute Muslims for medical treatment, marriage and employment. It is engaged in purchasing plots for commercial purposes and constructing office-cum-residential accommodation. Its sole source of income is the rent and lease amount on properties under tenancy. The Central Wakf Council also provides funds for activities organised by the council but administered by the board. I have covered a few institutions that do excellent work and constitute civil society in these areas. As the famous historian Irfan Habib says: "Civil society is like public opinion in ancient Greek society and helps people in various ways."

What is Wakf

According to the Hanafi Sect of Islamic Law, "It is the detention of specific things in the ownership of the Waqif or appropriator, and devoting its profits or usufruct to charity, the poor or other good objects."

Two elements are important in this definition:

(i)   The ownership of the Wakf remains after its creation;
(ii) Religious and pious purposes Muslim scholar Abu Yusuf identified three elements of Wakf;

(iii)   Ownership of God;

(iv)   The extinction of the founder's right;

(v)   Benefit to mankind;

However, Imam Mohammed said the 'rights of the Wakf do not cease in the property until he has appointed a Muttawalli and delivered its possession into their hands'.

The Mussalman Wakf Validating Act 1913 says "Wakf means the permanent dedication by a person professing the Mussalman faith of any property for any purpose recognised by Mussalman Law as religious, pious or charitable".

The Wakf Act 1954 defines Wakf as: "Wakf means the permanent dedication, by a person professing Islam, of any movable or immovable property for any purpose recognised by the Muslim Law as pious, religious or charitable".

How Wakf is created

The Muslim Law, as practiced in India, does not prescribe a specific method to create Wakf. However, there are four modes:

- Wakf by an act of 'in fervivos' (between living voices). It means persons can Wakf a portion of their property during their lifetime;

- Wakf can also be created by a will or Vasiyat;

- Wakf can be created during fatal illness (Marz-ul-maut). In this case, only 113 portions will be considered as Wakf;

- Most controversially, Wakf can be created by immemorial use. All historical mosques, tombs, graveyards are Wakf by this definition. We have two different positions on this issue.

In the NR Abdul Azeez vs Sundaresa Chettiar case (AIR 1993, Madras; 169), the Madras High Court held that no Muslim can be denied the right to offer prayers therein on the ground that the mosque fell into disuse long back. Therefore when the dilapidated structure was proved to be an old mosque, it became Wakf by use. However, in the Mohammed Ismail Faruqui vs Union of India case (AIR, 1994, SC 605), the Supreme Court held that where a mosque has been adversely possessed by non-Muslims, it lost its sacred character. Also, the state had power to acquire property under the Land Acquisition Act, 1984.

Wakf distinguished from Sadqah, Hiba and Trust

S.No.	Sadqah	Wakf
1	The legal estate, not merely the interest, is passed to the charity to be held by the trustees appointed by the donor.	The legal estate or ownership is not vested in the trustee or Muttawalli. It is transferred to God.
2	Both the corpus and usufruct are given away. Trustees can sell property.	Trustees cannot alienate the corpus of property, except with court permission or settlor's authorisation.
3	It is donation or gift.	It is an endowment.
	Hiba	**Wakf**
1	The dominion over the object passes from one human being to another.	The right of Waqif is extinguished and passes in favour of the Almighty.
2	Delivery of possession is essential.	In a Wakf in fervivos, no delivery of possession is essential. It is created by mere declaration of endowment.

3	No limitation with regard to object for which it is created.	Only for religious, charitable or pious purposes. Wakf for family purposes should also be for charity.
4	Property passes from one person to another, absolute right is transferred.	Right of Wakf extinguished, passes infavour of God, administration by an appointed Muttawalli. Beneficiaries have only the mentioned interest.
	Trust	**Wakf**
1	No religious motive necessary.	The motive is usually religious.
2	A trustee may be a beneficiary.	A settler, except in Hanafi law, cannot reserve benefit for himself.
3	Involves double ownership—equitable and legal. The property vests in a trustee.	Ownership of Waqif extinguished, vested in God.
4	Trustee has powers of alienation because heor she is the legal owner.	Muttawalli is a mere receiver and manager.
5	A trustee cannot demand remuneration.	Muttawalli may ask for remuneration.
6	It is not necessary that a trust be perpetual, irrevocable or inalienable.	Property is inalienable, irrevocable and perpetual.

Source: Aqil Ahmad, "Mohammedan Law", revised by Dr LA Khan (Allahabad: Central Law Agency, 2000).

Darul-Uloom,
Deoband, District Saharanpur, Uttar Pradesh

This great institution (established on 30 May 1866) was part of a larger ideological ferment against colonial modernity that emerged in the 19 century, especially among the ulema. Maulanas Qasim Nanautavi and Abid Hussain Deobandi played a key role in setting up what was at one level an attempt to redefine Islam for the prevailing historical situation and at another a symbol of protest against British colonial hegemony. These two are linked ideologically—for, the search for an Islamic answer to colonial modernity is distinguished by its nascent nationalism.

After 1857, the British started targeting madrassas for their perceived role in the rebellion. Maulana Nanotvi, who had participated in the 1857 action, wanted to form an institution that could produce true Indian Muslim ulema. Nationalist Islam was, thus, the very raison d'etre of the Deoband madrassa. Even during the movement for Pakistan, Deoband categorically rejected the Muslim League demand for a separate Muslim homeland and advocated Hindu-Muslim unity. This does not mean, however, that the madrassa ever compromised with its fundamental objective. It has been working, since inception, for the establishment of complete Shariat in Muslim society.

After the September 11 attacks, the Deoband madrassa attracted a lot of media attention. This was in the wake of talk that the erstwhile Taliban regime in Afghanistan subscribed to Deobandi ideology. Even Kashmiri terrorism was sought to be linked to Darul-Uloom. The madrassa had to brave this onslaught of negative perception. Maulana Qasim Usman Mansupuria, Pro Vice-Chancellor, Deoband, had to put it on record in an interview that the madrassa could not be held responsible per se for any kind of anti-national activity. He pinpointed the reason for this confusion—in the subcontinent, Deoband is recognised not only as a centre of religious education but also as a school of thought that had come to be known by its name, implying an orthodox attitude towards questions like Shariat, etc. If someone in Afghanistan is called Deobandi as a result of self-ascription or public image, it does not mean they are a student of Darul-Uloom. Deobandi, here, refers to an ideology that has far outstripped its eponymous madrassa and become coopted in political strategies of more recent vintage and reactionary content.

Darul-Uloom is among the best madrassas in the world for Islamic religious instruction, with six main departments (Arabic, Qirat, Diniyat, Ifta, Urdu, Calligraphy), besides courses in English, History, Geography and Civics. It has a huge and famous library, with 1.5 lakh-odd books on over 100 subjects in around 20 languages. All this is open to students of all age groups. There is no fixed age limit for admission. Students who are selected via a written entrance exam are provided free clothes, books and other material. Of a total strength of 4,500 students, only a small section pays tuition fees. Besides India, the quality Islamic training offered here attracts students from Afghanistan, China, Russia, Indonesia, Iran, South Africa, Saudi Arabia, Syria and Yemen. Over 300 teachers and 200 non-teaching staff cater to this throng.

Three elected committees run the administration here. The 21-member Majlis-e-Shura or apex managing body, which is assisted by the Majlis-e-Amila and the Majlis-e-Ilmia. The annual budget of around ₹6 crore is linked to an organised system of fundraising. Darul-Uloom has 32 safirs (representatives) who collect annual Zakat, Imbad, Fitrah and Sadqa from mosques all over India. It also receives contribution from like-minded organisations and

Early Origins in Religious Philanthropy

individuals abroad. All income expenditure details are published annually by Darul UIoom.

Jamiyatul Hidaya,
1618, Khijre ka Rasta, opposite Hidayat Masjid, near Sandra Bazar, Jaipur, Rajasthan

Coming into existence in 1976—as a late by-product of the anti-modern wave that engulfed Islam in colonial India—it is one of India's most prestigious madrassas. Unlike Darul-Uloom, Deoband, and Nadwatul Uloom, Lucknow, it goes an extra step to accommodate modem education. The idea is to raise new, aware community leadership from among ulema armed with modem tools and concepts. The institute advocates that ulema must engage actively with the political, moral and religious affairs of Indian Muslims. To this end, it believes merely setting up religious institutes will not suffice. An alim must be able to resolve uniquely modern social questions.

It recognises that the urban middle class does not wish to send its children to madrassas, owing to a general disenchantment over the quality of education. The shrinking job opportunities for alims generate a natural anxiety. The Jamiyatul Hidaya has designed its programme such that Muslims from all walks of life could maximise benefits—an approach that echoes its ideological position. Shah Hidayat Ali Saheb had initiated the movement for such a madrassa in the 1920s. His son, Shah Abdul Rahim Saheb, a critic of the Deoband approach, favoured a blend of Islamic and modem education to produce a kind of ulema that could withstand all anti-Islamic forces and pressures.

The institute does not tap the general public for money. Provisions from the family-run Maulana Abdul Rahim Education

Trust, special fundraising drives among affluent Muslims, fees from students and donations from state institutions make for an annual budget in the region of ₹2 crore. The family of Shah Hidayat Ali Saheb are still the main custodians. Abdul Rahim Saheb's sons, Fazal-ur-Rahim and Ziya-ur-Rahim, are the madrassa's principal and caretaker respectively. It offers courses in Diniyat (up to Alim stage), electrical and mechanical engineering, computers, infotech, etc. It also offers the NCERT syllabus from Class I to X and books from the Rajasthan Senior Secondary Course. Around 650 students reside in the madrassa, with 45 teachers and 25 non-teaching staff who are paid employees.

Al-Ameen
Hosur Road, Bangalore, Karnataka
Al-Ameen manages over 130 institutions in India. An exhaustive listing of its programmes, activities and achievements and description of its contributions for and commitment to the downtrodden in general and Muslims in particular requires a book in itself. It is a well-organised, target-oriented and dedicated presence in the fields of education, public health and banking. It is now involved in areas like development, legal advocacy, religious matters and sports and has plans to promote quality research in information technology and management.

The Al-Ameen movement started in 1967 when Dr Mumtaz Ahmed Khan, a medical practitioner, and other affluent Muslims established the Al-Ameen College in Bangalore. Its patron, the Al-Ameen Education Society, overcame initial financial troubles with the help of like-minded individuals and institutions. The Bangalore University granted affiliation to the Al-Ameen Arts, Commerce and Science College in 1967-66. In 1977, Al-Ameen set up its first financial institution, the Amanath Bank. The bank gave financial help to the education society. It also became a direct member of the clearance house and NRI and non-resident rupee (NRE) accounts were sanctioned. In 1984, Al-Ameen started its medical college. Since then, it has been financially self-sufficient and growing.

It now runs five primary schools, 15 high schools, three junior colleges, a degree college, a pharmacy college, a medical college, a dental college, an engineering college, a law college, a B.Ed. college, two technical training institutes, a scholarship fund and a library. It also has a cooperative bank, a non-interest finance corporation, a printing house and interests in the electric industry. It runs five hospitals in Karnataka and Gujarat, and one orphanage each in Karnataka and Kerala. Also, a women's hostel in Karnataka and a Haj house in Maharashtra.

Al-Ameen advocates a liberal secular image of Islam. This goes much beyond the good number of non-Muslims who study at its institutes. For instance, it has been encouraging ulema and intellectuals towards many ends, like promoting many Shariat courts in Karnataka. Dr Khan favours creating conditions in which Muslims can solve their disputes without going to formal courts. Al-Ameen is also a consistent votary of Islamic banks. It believes Islamic tenets and modern financial principles can be blended to form viable financial institutions. Al-Ameen has also been associating with the Islamic Development Bank. The Amanath Bank is the outcome of this open liberal outlook, which has earned it credibility within the community. Its education society speaks of an Islamic culture in its institutions, but this Islamism is a humanitarian impulse. It also lays much emphasis on female education. Its vigorous advocacy all over India on this issue is complemented by the institutions it has set up exclusively for women and by special scholarships and awards (like the Bibi Khadija Award). At the fundamental level, it concerns itself with quality primary education because it believes progress is incumbent on eliminating ignorance among Muslims. Such focused social action has ensured a diversity of domains of activity and also a geographical spread: Karnataka, Kerala, Maharashtra, Gujarat and even Delhi where it initiated a scholarship programme in 1996-97 with the help of the Hamdard Education Society. Besides self-generated resources, state funding accrues from the fact of its affiliation to various universities. There is also a flow of foreign funds and involvement in joint ventures with foreign universities, especially vis-a-vis infotech.

Muslim Association
Thiruvananthapuram, Kerala

This was established in 1966 by a section of affluent Muslims of Kerala, with the stated aim of uplifting deprived people in general and Muslims in particular, especially via education. Its charter of activities reflects a liberal Islam stance. Bylaws stipulate that anyone over 18, regardless of caste, creed, colour or religion, can enlist as member (though only four of the current strength of 1,100 are non-Muslim). The target group is clearly the Muslim middle-class-despite a rhetorical claim of being for the Umma (the community), it does not accommodate fisherfolk, the most deprived among Kerala Muslims. Politically, it is pro-Muslim League and functions as a pressure group.

Its institutions are popular among non-Muslims. The computer centre MACIT which is affiliated with the Indira Gandhi National Open University (IGNOU), Madurai Kamaraj University and SITECH, is a reputed institute in Thiruvananthapuram. It also runs two men's and one women's hostel, a middle school for boys, a CBSE-affiliated primary public school, the Thampanoor mosque and a cultural centre, musafir khana and a crèche. Besides publishing literature on Islamic history and culture, it offers scholarships to select poor students, runs self-employment schemes, coaching classes for competitive exams, and gives medical aid. The association relies on public collections, foreign funds (e.g., from the Islamic Development Bank, Jeddah) and government aid. It does not formally collect Zakat but accepts donations.

Beema Palli Muslim Jamaat
Thiruvananthapuram, Kerala

The Beema Palli is the second largest and oldest mosque in the city. Arab traders who started coming to Kerala in the seventh century forged good rapport with the locals and also propagated Islam among them. Historically, these Muslims established 18 mosques in different parts of Kerala. Beema Palli is one of them. Also said to be the shrine of a Sufi, its activities extend beyond the usual rituals and take in social and educational work. The Jamaat, a registered society, offers membership only to Muslims though the shrine is open to all devotees. The imam of the mosque is the functional head or president, besides whom the Jamaat executive committee has 30 elected members. The Jamaat appoints the mujabeer, who take care of the shrine's maintenance and rituals. Every Thursday a free langar is organised for all. An annual urs is also held. Apart from this, the Jamaat runs five madrassas which offer Hafiz, Qari, Alim and Mufti degrees courses. It has a government-aided high school and a few small institutions exclusively working for Muslims. Chadhawa is a major source of funds for the Beema Palli. On an average, 500 devotees visit the shrine daily. The Jamaat, which does not collect Zakat, also gets financial help from a section of rich Muslims.

Palayam Muslim Jamaat
Thiruvananthapuram, Kerala

Palayam Palli is one of the oldest mosques of Thiruvananthapuram and also the biggest. Built by Nawab Mohammed Ali (1748-1795) to provide accommodation to Muslim soldiers, the mosque went on to become a hub of social activities. The prime task of the Jamaat—an unregistered society with 2,600 members of the Shaifi sect—is the upkeep and development of the mosque. It supports its poorer members and, for the public, it runs a general hospital and an Arabic madrassa. The Jamaat, which has an elected executive committee, collects a monthly subscription of ₹5 from members. It also receives donations from outside. The Jamaat does not collect Zakat as this money cannot be used for the maintenance of mosques. Other forms of charity like Sadqa and Hiba are common. An interesting source of funds is marriage fee. The Jamaat changes ₹500 from the groom and ₹300 from the bride as marriage fee.

Darul-Uloom Nadwatul Ulema,
Lucknow, Uttar Pradesh

Set up in 1893, the Nadwatul Ulema was a sign of the reformism that characterised a certain kind of response to the socio-political situation of the day. This section of Sunni Hanafi ulema, led by figures like Maulana Mohammed Ali Mangeri, sought to harmonise the different streams of thought among Muslims. The Nadwatul Uloom was established later to buttress this spirit with a platform to raise reformist ulema.

The Nadwatul Ulema, which adopted a secular line during the freedom struggle, favoured changes in the Islamic theological syllabi to bring it in line with modern conditions and the community's cultural progress within it. It also stood for a fresh appraisal of the Shariat's principles and injunctions to keep it in conformity with the fundamental guidance of the Quran and Sunnat and sensitise it to modern questions. For this task, it wanted to establish a central library in north India that could serve as a focal point of research in Islam for a line of preachers who would have a deep knowledge of textual Islam and a keen appreciation of the prevailing situation. Such a line of ulema would be able to make meaningful interventions, according to this view.

It saw virtue in integrating the fundamentals of the faith and the ever-changing values of human knowledge, or in bringing harmony to the various Ahl-e-Sunnat schools. This approach visualised Islamic sciences as living, evolving and progressive—and, since knowledge was subject to the law of change and reform, it was essential that the education system too should evolve with the needs of the Islamic Millat. Besides, it also focuses on an agenda revolving around reformist social action.

Its courses in theology span from primary to Alimiyat (graduation), Fazilat (post-graduation) and Taknik (doctorate) stages. English, Hindi, History, Math and Sciences are also taught. Besides, it offers a five-year course in Arabic literature, one each in Islamic thought and comparative religions and teachers training. No fee is charged from the 4,000-odd students provided free board and lodging at its different branches in Uttar Pradesh. About 1,000 students are awarded stipends. Nadwa has 131 teachers and 103 non-teaching staff.

The Uloom has a grand library, housed in a five-storey building, which scholars from various universities in India and abroad visit for its rare collection of 1.5 lakh books. It also has a well-maintained section holding over 5,000 manuscripts in Arabic, Persian, Urdu and Hindi and an English section that has over 4,000 books on sundry modern subjects.

Given its overarching reformist concern, Nadwa has set up various departments, the most notable being the department of social reform whose central office in Lucknow coordinates with branches all over India. The department of Fiqh and Ifta i.e., Islamic law and question and answers, at one level trains muftis (legists, experts on law) and qazis (judges). At another, as a centre of scholarship, it answers queries received from all over the world—with citations, references and precedence—on the applicability of Islamic law. Nadwa also has many research academies and institutions that publish works of outstanding merit on Islamic faith, history and philosophy, etc. One is Darul Musannefin, which functions out of Azamgarh as an independent organisation.

The Majlis-e-Shafat-o-Nashriyat publishes a monthly journal in Arabic, Al-B 'aas-al-Islami, which carries articles by well-known writers from India and the Arab world. It has readership in the subcontinent and also the Arab countries where it has acquired a respectable status as among the best of its genre. The Majlis-e-Tahqiqat-o-Nashriyat-e-Islam, or the Academy of Islamic Research and Publication, born in 1959 with Maulana Syed Abu Hasan Ali Nadwi as president, began by producing Islamic literature in English, Arabic, Urdu and Hindi and has so far brought out 227 books, of which over a hundred have seen several reprints.

A mohtamim (principal) is in charge of the Uloom administration. Its management committee is a fixed-tenure elected body, consisting of distinguished ulema, altogether 63, drawn from all over India. An honorary nazim (secretary general), assisted by a motarnad-i-talim (academic advisor) and motarnad-i-maliyat (treasurer), is in charge of day-to-day management of the organisation, which has an annual budget of ₹4 crore. Nadwa receives Zakat and donations, including from the Arab world. It has FCRA (Foreign Contribution Regulation Act, 2010) and income tax exemption.

Jamaat-e-Islami Hind
Bazar Chitli Qabar, Jama Masjid, Delhi

Established in 1939, this is India's second largest Muslim organisation. The Jamaat faced a major split in 1947 when the Jamaat-e-Islami Pakistan was born. Despite its founder Moulana Abul Al-Modudi too opting for Pakistan, his basic ideas on the relationship between the faith and the polity continue to influence the Indian Jamaat which accepted him as ultimate guide. Modudi was a critic of the national movement. In his opinion, after independence, political authority would simply pass into the hands of the Hindu majority. He cherished the notion of Hukumat-e-Elahiya (the government of God, in other words a theological state).

Modudi set up his first organisation, the Darul-Islam, at Pathankot in 1938 with the help of a few big Muslim landlords. This did not attract people much in a Punjab that was witnessing the high noon of the Muslim League's popularity. On 26 August 1941, Modudi constituted the Jamaat at Lahore. He challenged Jinnah's political mobilisation and argued that the Pakistan movement should be based on radical Islam rather than western liberalism.

During 1947-50, after Modudi left India to become a mainstream figure in Pakistani politics, the Jamaat here entered a new, uncertain phase. In 1954, the Uttar Pradesh government imposed a ban on its activities and arrested its senior leaders. The incident brought a new kind of political awareness. Adjusting to the changing political conditions in the 1950s, the Jamaat published its constitution. This afforded the Jamaat a safe, valid political space. It only spoke of striving towards the complete din (religion) in India, a mere statement of orthodoxy. Of course, it is debatable whether such a state is achievable without establishing Hukumat-e-Elahiya.

The Jamaat's target group has always been the educated Muslim. This explains its propaganda strategy of relying on a variety of published literature. This mobilised the people and also helped the Jamaat's finances. The Markazi Maktaba Islamia, its publication wing, is still performing both functions.

In 1975, during Emergency, the Jamaat was again banned. It was then that it opened up politically and interacted with other major political parties and allowed its members to cast votes in elections. After the Babri Masjid demolition, the Jamaat was banned for a third time in independent India. This ban was lifted in 1994.

The Jamaat's organisational structure is rigid; something sought to be justified by references to the holy khilafat system. Article 10 of the constitution defines its various levels: central, regional and local. All of them have four organs: a 10-member elected shura, an amir nominated as its head, and an advisory council and secretary. The amir at the centre is the Jamaat's head and has no fixed tenure. Article 6 of its constitution explains that every citizen of India, male or female, and irrespective of community or race, is eligible for membership. But this secular stance is qualified by Article 6(1), which says "a member has to understand the kalima Ilaha Illah Muhammadur Rasulallah (There is no God but Allah and Muhammad is his true Prophet)" and believe it, this is notably the first step in the process of bait or accepting Islam. Thus, implicitly, a prospective member of the Jamaat has to be Muslim.

The Jamaat's approach to the status of Muslims was intriguing. Before Independence, it represented itself as the most radical

Muslim outfit. It rejected the Muslim League's constitutional minorityism, which was vying for a separate state via constitutional politics and direct action. But its own ambiguous approach offered no alternative. Post-1950, the Jamaat reformulated its strategy. Without participating in active politics, it evolved a stance that emphasised the interests of educated Muslims. The Jamaat runs a few schools. Other details of its programmes, except the publication of literature and the activities of the SIMI, are not available. It has a huge campus in Delhi. It also collects Zakat for its activities via the Baitul-mall.

Jamiat Ulema-e-Hind
1, Bahadur Shah Zafar Marg, New Delhi
The nationalist ulema started with armed resistance, but repeated failure motivated them to revise their approach. Subsequently, they joined the struggle for freedom. In November 1919, the revolutionary ulema, on the occasion of the Khilafat conference, decided to constitute their own organisation—this was designated as the Jamiat Ulema-i-Hind. Mufti-e-Azam Maulana Kifayatullah was elected as first president. This body stood firmly against Muslim communalism and opposed the demand for Partition. After Independence, it resisted all forms of Hindu and Muslim bigotry. Its chief concerns revolved around securing an equal status, legitimate civil rights, justice and adequate representation for Muslims. To this can be added protection of identity and heritage; promoting social, educational and religious reform; reframing syllabi for the present age; and the general propagation of Islamic thought.

To fulfill these objectives, Jamiat has 18 state-level offices all over India and various associated bodies. With a direct link with the Darul-Uloom, Deoband, it is one of the most prestigious organisations in India in the field of education. (Teachers at Deoband are paid by the Jamiat.) It runs 300 primary schools all over India, benefiting 60,000-odd children a year. Its secular-religious approach is reflected in its pedagogy, blending the best Islamic training with modem education. The Muslim Fund, Deoband, provides interest-free credit through 318 branches. The ITI, Deoband, also benefits 200 students every year. It has six mobile dispensaries and is planning to establish two hospitals, six TB and leprosy centres and a paramedic training institute.

Jamiat is also known for its humanitarian work after all disasters: natural or manmade. For instance, its relief work for riot victims in Gujarat was preceded by a huge Gujarat Earthquake Relief Project. It ran five relief camps at Anjar, Bhuj, Kotda, Bhachau, and Vankaner, and is part of a joint front constructing 3,358 houses in 13 villages. It is also actively working for the Jamiat Children Village at Anjar. This multi-dimensional model village will have a secondary school and a women's centre. Besides, Jamiat is planning a vocational centre and a girl's hostel in Bhuj. Total budget: US $1,852,702.

In 1991, Jamiat conducted a nationwide reform campaign. The issues it highlighted span the range from social to economic: dowry and divorce law, the privileges of women in Islam, the reformist thrust and content of the holy texts, problems in adapting to information technology. Its leaders have been an active voice against communalism of all types, within Parliament and outside, seeking to secure the support of secular political elements and intellectuals to resist growing communal tendencies among the majority. In all this, Jamiat goes beyond mere advocacy—whenever information about a riot is received, its central office informs the chief minister and central authorities and enlists their support for initiating relief work. It takes steps to protect life and property, and towards rehabilitation. Efforts are also made to secure rightful compensation.

This role also has a decidedly political edge, natural in a situation where, as Jamiat says, Muslims tend to suffer heavy losses in riots yet shoulder much of the blame. Jamiat sends deputations for spot studies, which go into detailed reports that have often publicised facts when the local administration did not. A report on Godhra was one such. Jamiat also takes legal steps to secure the release of innocents. When a commission of inquiry looks into a riot, Jamiat appears as a party to identify the culprits and present the sequence of events.

In 1963, Jamiat came under the Societies Registration Act. It has FCRA and income tax exemption. The Jamiat trust, with a seven-member board, looks after the finances. Jamiat receives Zakat and other religious charity from India and abroad, especially the Middle East and the UK.

Anjuman Minhaj-e-Rasool
254512, Tiraha Behram Khan, Daryaganj, Delhi

A social organisation-cum-pressure group, the Anjuman was set up in 1988 by a group of young alims from a Tabliqi Jamaat background inspired by its chair, Maulana Syed Athar Hussain Dehlvi. Secular Islamic nationalism—built around tolerance, communal amity and social and religious reform— is its core ideology. Among many other valuable contributions, its intervention in Kashmir is notable. Exercised over the overt linking of religion with secessionism, it sought to give an Islamic answer to foreign-funded terrorism. In its publications, it consistently emphasised Kashmir's Rishi-Sufi tradition. It has now commissioned a research on Kashmir's historical monuments, to evolve a people-centric conservation policy.

Among its many titles is a biographical volume on the Sufis-Rishis, a critical study of Islamic fundamentalist organisations and Maulana Abul Kalam Azad's thought. It conducts seminars, workshops and colloquia on themes like women and Islam, the question of Imamat (leadership), Gandhi and Indian ulema, the Vedic tradition and saffronisation of education, and religion in the third sector. It also convened the first-ever summit of the Shankaracharya and Muslim organisations on Ayodhya and other issues.

The Anjuman has branches all over India. Its majlis-e-shura an elected body with four women members-appoints the Amir (chair) who names state-level chiefs in a consultative process. Its chief source of income is the Islamic and other literature it publishes. The Anjuman, which also plans to come out with a newspaper, has applied for FCRA and income tax exemption.

Dargah Shahdara Sharif
Poonch, Jammu and Kashmir

A key representative of Kashmiri culture and its accommodative Islam, Dargah Shahdara Sharif in the Rajouri district of Jammu—which houses the shrine of Pir Ghulam Shah Badshah, of the Sunni Qadri sect—is a state-managed pilgrim centre like the Ajmer dargah. The state of J&K appoints an administrator to manage the dargah and its Wakf. When Kashmir was blighted by terrorism, the Shahdara Sharif proved that Kashmiris groomed in the Rishi-Sufi stream are not natural followers of fundamentalist Islam. The number of devotees at the dargah has never dipped despite repeated militant attacks in the area.

The dargah has income tax exemption and J&K rules govern the application of FCRA. The donation box collection is its main source of income. The Urs is an event that helps generate income with the annual collection now nearing ₹1 crore. The dargah committee, constituted by the administrator, is in charge of developing the centre. It organises a daily langar for 5,000-odd pilgrims and has built a 100-room musafir khana. The dargah also offers financial help to 33 madrassas in Rajouri and gives pension to the elderly and handicapped.

Jamia Hamdard
Hamdard Nagar, Delhi

Literally the one who empathises, Hamdard is not an unknown name in India. It is a famous centre of Unani medicine, which produces Rooh Afza, India's largest selling sharbat, among other brands. It is also a leading Muslim philanthropic organisation and a presence in education, with a deemed university recognised by the University.

Its founder-patriarch Hakim Abdul Hameed a nationalist and friend of Maulana Abul Kalam Azad who opposed the idea of Pakistan is a symbol of Muslim contribution to science. Cohabitation had produced a unique synthesis between Unani medicine and Ayurveda.

When allopathy relegated both to the margins, Hakim saheb's response was to modernise Unani with new research bolstering a traditional knowledge system. His exertions bore fruit soon as Hamdard became a household name.

In 1948, Hakim saheb declared his dawakhana as a Wakf. Since then, a portion of its income has gone into philanthropy. In 1962, Hakim saheb set up the pioneering Institute of History of Medicine and Medical Research. A year later followed the Indian Institute of Islamic Studies. Their success brought forth more institutions: the Hamdard College of Pharmacy in 1972, the Hamdard Tibbia College in 1973, the 150-bed Majeedia Hospital (which offers treatment in Unani as well as modem medicine) in 1982 and the Rufaida School of Nursing in 1984. India's best medical colleges now recognise its Bachelor of Unani Medicine and Surgery (BUMS) course, in no small measure due to the modem facilities and an approach built around the contemporary relevance of research that supports it.

In 1989, the University Grants Committee recognised the success of these institutions which offer undergraduate, postgraduate and doctoral courses and declared Jamia Hamdard a deemed university. It now has six faculties (Islamic Studies and Social Sciences, Management and Information Technology, Medicine, Nursing, Pharmacy and Science), each engaged in teaching and research. The Hakim Mohammad Saeed library is perhaps India's most reputed library on Unani medicine and related Islamic history, with over a lakh books and unique manuscripts. The Hamdard Education Society, a sister organisation, runs a public school and a coaching centre.

In 1964, the Hamdard National Foundation was set up to receive and disburse income received from the Hamdard (Wakf) Laboratories for charitable work in education and medical relief. The UGC and the Islamic Development Bank also help the Hamdard Foundation. The university has FCRA clearance and income tax exemption. In 2000-01, Jamia Hamdard's total expenditure was ₹15.83 crore, inclusive of the self-financing courses. The foundation gave a grant of ₹3.5 crore. A deficit of ₹6.53 crore was met by internal resource generation such as fees and rentals.

Zakat Foundation of India
D-208, God's Grace Girls School, Abul Fazal Enclave, Jamia Nagar, Delhi

The Zakat Foundation of India (ZFI) was established specifically to systematise Zakat collection. The director, Syed Zafar Mehmud, and others took up this task to channelise community resources for wider social development, believing it to be a neglected area in India. It works at three levels to organise the Zakat system. At the first, members spread awareness about its importance as a religious and social act according to the Sharia. Then, it has instituted a modern, transparent system for collecting Zakat. Donors can deposit cheques (no cash) in ZFI accounts at the Janata Cooperative Bank, Old Delhi, (Zakat account no. 6291), and at the Jamia Cooperative Bank at Jamia Millia Islamia (Zakat account no. 3432). ZFI has a separate account for imdad and sadqa at the former bank (account no. SBF-16). At the third level, it distributes the Zakat among poor students, widows and others. It spends no sum on its own organisational and administrative functions. All ZFI members work on an honorary basis, dividing the expenses. In 2000-2001, the ZFI could collect only a meagre ₹54,000, which was distributed in Delhi and Lucknow. It has applied for FCRA and income tax exemption and hopes to better its record.

Dargah Khwaja Moinuddin Chishti
Ajmer, Rajasthan

Khwaja Moinuddin Chishti is among the greatest Sufis of India. His dargah is an arch symbol of Indianised Islam and the unifying, syncretic strand in the Hindu-Muslim cultural encounter. Moinuddin is believed to have been born in a town called Sanjor in Central Asia, migrating to India in 1165 AD to be a staunch partisan of the poor and destitute and a voice against exploitation. After his death, his khanqah was converted into his dargah. Ever since, people from all walks of life, irrespective of caste, class or religion, visit this shrine, offer tributes and partake of the langar. The offerings, in cash or kind, are called nazar or nazrana. On the annual Urs eve, the numbers rise to millions.

In time, however, a body of superstition replaced the true spirit of the Khwaja's message. The huge pool of devotees (and, consequently, nazrana) prompted many parties to say they were the legal and religious heirs. To deal with the situation, the government appointed a committee in 1949, chaired by Justice Ghulam Hassan of the Allahabad High Court, to report on the dargah affairs. On the basis of its recommendation, that the Centre empower a committee to administer, control and manage the dargah, Parliament passed the Dargah Khwaja Saheb Act, 1955 (this was amended first in 1964, then in 1983). It stated that the endowment administered by the dargah committee includes the Dargah Khwaja Saheb, all buildings and movable property within its boundaries, the dargah jagir, all attached shops and buildings, all other property and all income derived from any source whatsoever dedicated to the dargah.

The dargah committee, comprising five to nine nominated members, is assisted by the nizim. Apart from administration and maintenance, the committee handles the Urs. It also runs 11 primary schools in rural Rajasthan, a computer centre and coaching centre in Ajmer, besides providing langar and medical aid to the poor and sundry services. The dargah's accounts are audited by the Accountant General, Rajasthan. In 1998-99, the committee received ₹1.12 crore from all sources.

Ulema Council, Hasanath Primary School
Rudrapur, Uddham Singh Nagar, Uttarakhand

The council was established in November 2001 after Maulana Zahid Raza Rizvi, an active member of the Uttar Pradesh Haj committee, organised the ulema of Uttarakhand. It aims to give the new state's Muslims a blend of Islamic and modern education and promote harmony among the various sects to establish a joint front of all ulema. With minority rights as another thrust area, it is also engaged in promoting religious and social reform. The council has been working against the dowry system and striving for Shariat rights to women.

To pursue these aims, the council has established two primary schools. One is the Jamiat ul Hasanath, Rudrapur, which also houses its head office. It caters to 140-odd students with funds generated from the local community. The other school, Madrassa-i-Shaya-tul-Hag in Dehradun, is a religious institution. This is also a self-sustaining school but the 95 students, unlike at Hasanath, pay a fee of ₹35 a month. The council, which collects Zakat every year in the month of Ramadan, has applied for Foreign Contribution Regulation Act (FCRA) and income tax exemption.

Hasanath Education Society
43, Dickenson Road, Bangalore

Adam Hajee Ebrahim Sait and HM Ismail floated the society in 1971, prioritising women's education and addressing those sections of society which could not afford regular schooling. The Hasanath Pre-University College for women started with just 12 students. At present, the society runs several institutions in Bangalore, including the Hasanath Institute of Management, Hasanath Learning and Resource Centre, Hasanath Pre-University College for men and the Hasanath Academy of Management Studies. Karnataka has accorded recognition to these colleges, as has the UGC—both are also major sources of funds, along with the Amanath Bank and public collection. The state Wakf board also gives land in Bangalore to its different institutes, which offer courses in arts, science, commerce, computer science, business management, and job-oriented areas like tourism and travel management. Around 2,500 students study in Hasanath institutes, only 40 per cent of them Muslims. The society prepares students for competitive exams and also aids in employment with a placement cell.

Issues and debates

Despite fundamental differences, Islamic organisations share a few basic concerns like welfare of Muslims in India. This imposes a few formal similarities, even in the different solutions they strive for. All organisations taken for study are registered although only the bigger five benefit from FCRA. The rest are either applicants or diffident about placing their status on record. (This last is a function of their placement vis-a-vis the state, vitiated after September 11 and the Gujarat riots.)

Only seven are entitled for income tax exemption (again the small bodies are outside the ambit). Although all the surveyed organisations audit their accounts internally and externally, funding is a tricky issue and insistent field queries come up against evasive response. The following facts are relevant: only the dargahs and mosques rely on zayareen and namazis, all collect membership fee (an important source, given their size), 12 collect money from affluent Muslims, 11 from general Muslims, three from non-Muslims and eight from the state. Only 11 generate their own income.

In terms of expenditure, all the surveyed organisations are

linked with education, only eight with the health sector (this reveals the community's priority) and seven are engaged in advocating the re-establishment of the Shariat. As many as 14 do relief and rehabilitation work, often irrespective of caste, class and religion. Nine organisations conduct or support Islamic research theological or sociological. As regards the perceived crisis facing the Muslims in India, 15 believe the lack of representation in legislatures, 'A' grade services, business, premier education, police and other sensitive services is its most visible reflection. Eleven feel with the communal atmosphere in India, a sense of deprivation has choked the Muslim mind, a key take-off point for their entire social project. Many attribute the systematic exclusion of Muslims from various public spheres to policy. Most, except a few in the south, associate the crisis also with the decline in Urdu—also that a package of legal reforms can protect minority culture. Seven suggest reservations for Muslims as a way out. There is yet no enthusiasm to work with the emerging Third Sector most prefer a relation to Islamic social precepts rather than modem socio-economic ones.

Of the 18 organisations working in education, 13 are engaged at the primary level of education including small madrassas and schools run by dargah committees. Ten are involved at the secondary level and seven each at the higher secondary and college level. Five support higher studies. Only one calls for a purely Islamic approach, most prefer different blends with modern elements.

A quantitative analysis like this, besides the field constraints that affects the inflow of information, has to be accompanied by a keen appreciation of the sense of alienation of the community and the historical moments in response to which these organisations cropped up. To achieve a cooperative unity of different social actors, the difference has to be respected and accepted. The NGO sector has to rethink its position on religious organisations to forge linkages with them (and, crucially, among them) and bring them under the fold of meaningful distributive justice in the modern sense. Especially because their geographical span tends to be limited, and at the popular level, the multiple overlaps of caste, class, gender and ethnic identities allow for a more rounded reception of volunteerism than pure, abstract Islam.

For, despite being perhaps the first religion to put the principle of democracy into practice, its appropriation by dominant groups converted it into a highly closed, authoritative religion. We should seek a return to the original emphasis on human freedom and the glorious assimilation it went through in India. The local organisations, with their secular and sophisticated outlook, represent a sort of people's Islam. It is at this level that a democratic movement can be initiated within the community with dialogue, an attempt to redefine Islam as an ideology of liberation and a formation of an open people's front for transforming the elite philanthropic discourse into a people's resolve. I am highlighting Wakf and its details as few understand them and many consider it as closed and authoritative and refusing to be part of the mainstream.

GIVING IN CHRISTIANITY

Christian giving is almost tautology: the two words not just share a fuzzy border in the manner of neighbourly concepts, they largely inhabit a shared turf, so tightly meshed are the ideas of philanthropy and being Christian. Logically, this must derive back to its pure embryonic stage, predating the birth of the organised church and its adoption of the ideal of giving as a practical instrument for its growth. Giving as praxis comes to fruition with Christ himself, who realises himself in this tradition as the first philanthropist. Here, in this incipient stage itself, are fused our twin ideas—drawing its stuff from the figure of Christ on the crucifix. From this early scenario, dating back to the story of the coming of the Holy Spirit, to the followers of Jesus gathered after his tragic death, his resurrection and ascension, the various strands attain concretion. In the Bible, the book of Acts (2:4) elaborates: "All who believed were together and had all things in common. They would sell their possessions and goods and distribute the proceeds to all, as any had need". If the early Christians had recourse to a shared tenet or credo to practically confront their hard circumstances, it was this self same ideal. They shared their possessions to help each other and the wider community. They distributed food to widows and those in need on a daily basis. Paul, a great leader in this new movement, set an example: " ... we must support the weak, remembering the words of the Lord Jesus, for he himself said 'it is more blessed to give than to receive".

The commitment to giving, to helping others, and to being concerned about those who are weak—those who face deprivation spiritually, emotionally or merely financially, a notion that even got extended to those who suffer political deprivation in the modern sense—was thus rooted in the life and teachings of Jesus, in the scriptures and also in Jewish tradition. The Old and New Testaments offer ample evidence, if any was needed, of the scriptural basis of this tradition.

This fundamental benevolence even now defines the very mode of Christian activity, over and above the historically complex nature of its presence in many parts of the world. Transference may be said to have occurred, in proceeding from concept to praxis and towards organised religion, in which ideal has transformed itself into modality. In Christianity, this has meant carrying forward the desire to serve, to help others and to give, in multifarious activities Christian institutions became involved in running hospitals, orphanages, schools, housing trusts, charity work and so on. This has also been referred to as the diaconal ministry, where the church has formally run institutes, services and taken care of those who were hungry, weak, sick, in prison and in need. This concept is also with the missionary movement as Christians opened schools and hospitals, and worked through the developing countries a role that no doubt progressed in step with colonial expansion. But activities that accompanied the church's expansion, in many ways, became historical interventions in the socio-economic biographies of many regions of the world. Services of the traditional sort—in health, education and charity, etc. became enmeshed with not just modern relief work but the process of development itself. The church, despite all those who look askance at its near-biological instinct for self-preservation and propagation, was something no critic would deny a genuinely transformative presence.

Since World War II, many European and North American churches have formed special agencies to respond to the different needs of peoples and countries, especially those that arose out of the deeply deranging effects of war. For example, work with refugees, in reconstruction and with the rebuilding of society first in Europe and then working through the world, developed into the remit of Christian Aid.

Sponsored by 40 churches in Britain and Ireland, it now works in over 60 countries, pouring resources into emancipating people from debilitating circumstances. Today, Christian Aid emphasises its purpose as being "to expose the scandal of poverty, contribute to its eradication and to be prophetic in challenging the systems, structures and processes that work against the interest of those who have been made poor or marginalised". Christian Aid continues to support many agencies in the voluntary sector in India and has been considered to be part of the western missionary movement.

The place of the poor in the Bible

Turn to any major concordance of the Bible and you will find that the word poor appears many hundreds of times. Modern-day exegetists have pointed out that one in sixteen verses of the New Testament is about the poor, so is one in ten verses in Luke's gospel and one in every five in the book of James. It is evidently a concept central to the Christian doctrine, but it calls for circumspection lest one mistake the poor to be a freely occurring natural category. Such a fallacy, sadly not infrequently held, is attributable only to intellectual laziness, it has no scriptural basis.

The recurring emphasis on the special status of the poor can be traced to Jesus' teaching, its roots firmly planted in the Hebrew scriptures in which he was immersed. It is a message doubly reinforced—that we will be judged by the way we treat the poor and that, if we are ourselves poor, or if we make ourselves poor, we will be especially blessed. A qualifying clause needs to be introduced here to clarify this emphasis. In the Old Testament, the Hebrew word often used for poor is most accurately translated as poor, deprived and oppressed. This is crucial. For, poverty is never attributed to fate or chance, but to active human injustice. When God freed his people at the time of the Exodus they were themselves slaves—the poor and afflicted. Moses heard the voice of God from the burning bush: "I have seen the affliction of my people who are in Egypt, and have heard their cry because of their taskmasters; I know their sufferings, and I have come down to deliver them out of the hand of the Egyptians." (Ex. 3:7-8)

However, as Ron Sider has pointed out in his classic study Rich Christians in an Age of Hunger, the Israelis soon discovered that Yahweh's passion for justice was a double-edged weapon. When they were the oppressed, it led to their freedom. "But when they became the oppressors, it led to their destruction". Yahweh chose the prophets to deliver the bad news. Amos saw the rich "trample the head of the poor into the dust of the earth" (Amos 2:7). He observed that the affluent lifestyle of the rich was built on the oppression of the poor (6:1-70). He forecast the destruction of the northern kingdom, and so it happened. In turn, Isaiah and Jeremiah warned of the destruction of Judah: "Woe to those who decree ... to turn aside the needy from justice and to rob the poor of my people of their right..." (Is 10: 1-4)

The Hebrew scriptures show us how God actively sided with the poorest. The Psalms, which formed the minds of Jews and Christians alike, are distinctively prayers for the poor. "For the needy shall not always be forgotten, and the hope of the poor shall not perish forever", says Psalm 9. "As for me, I am poor and needy; but the Lord takes thought for me. Thou art my help and my deliver; do not tarry, a my God" (Ps. 40.17)

Jesus begins his early ministry by declaring himself heir to this tradition. He quotes from Isaiah:

- The spirit of the Lord is upon me
- Because he has anointed me to bring good news to the poor
- He has sent me to proclaim release to the captives
- And recovery of sight to the blind
- To let the oppressed go free
- To proclaim the year of the Lord's favour. (Lk. 4:18-19)

It is possible to interpret this passage metaphorically and to speak of the spiritually poor and the spiritually blind. However, the context from which the Old Testament quotation is taken would have left his listeners in no doubt. It is physical oppression and captivity from which Jesus, like Yahweh, promises freedom, just as it is when in Mathew 11:2-6, he told John's disciples—again in the words of Isaiah—that he healed the sick and brought good news to the poor. Jesus was acting, in the words of Ernest Fuchs, "in God's stead". He was a figure of power, announcing God's salvation for those denied it by earthly authorities. He poured scorn on religious and ethical codes that deny wholeness. As in the Old Testament, Jesus' message is a benediction on the poor. One of the beatitudes is translated by Luke as "Blessed are you who are poor, for yours is the kingdom of God". The semantic confusion on the very object of philanthropy, motivated doubtless by self-interest, continued. In the Middle Ages, it was argued that there needed to be both rich and poor in the economy of God's plan—the poor as objects of the rich's charity, offering the rich a way to earn eternal salvation. Since then the poor and the rich have moved further apart, even within the church. There continues, as Richard Harries points out, to be an excess of Christian individualism, as against a social ethic—a bias towards love (which assists the immediate needs of a few) as against justice (which addresses the future needs of many).

Justice and equality

A genuine answer to this riddle, and the only one that offers modern Christian philanthropy scope for self-validation, is to return to the values of the early Church: "God may only be done if amid all the complications and ambiguities we act to some extent as if in reality the wealth of the world is common wealth: as if it were given equally to all ... ". Christians need to respond to the poverty, injustice and inequality in the world and to their root causes, where all are made poorer when any are left out. At Christian Aid, a kernel belief is that "God hopes and works for a new earth where all shall be included in the feast of life". Simply put, Christian giving is now more than just giving money to good causes and abdicating further responsibility. For some time, the ecumenical response was to speak of 'the option for the poor'. However, if poverty is a scandal—as Christian Aid says in its newly published corporate plan—it is now less an option than a necessity. The voice of the poor must be paramount, not only in theology but also in hard-nosed development issues. For one, northern Christians always risk sentimentalising the condition of the poor, much as they are inclined to sentimentalise Jesus as the poor Suffering Servant and ignore the figure of authority who promised to liberate the poor. Recovering the lost emancipatory potential of the Christian doctrine has to be made integral to all organised work in public education, fundraising, campaigning and global advocacy.

The worldwide church today

The World Council of Churches (WCC) has served the ecumenical movement since 1948 as a place for reflection, cooperation, service and advocacy in areas of concern for the disadvantaged and marginalised. Its service agency CICARWS, the Commission on Inter-Church Aid, Refuge and World Service has been working with and through the churches and their specialised agencies (such as Christian Aid) in relief and development. Over the years a shift in style and emphasis from relief and helping others—to more long-term development, solidarity and helping others to help themselves—has been developed. Today, there is a desire to look more at the root causes of poverty, injustice and discrimination and to campaign for change. The WCC recognises that its work was about "carrying God's mercy into a merciless world". This required Christians to integrate compassion and service with a commitment to support the struggles for justice, inclusion and dignity for all; linking the love of neighbours to the whole agenda of justice, peace, and the integrity of creation. Christian giving was not just about identifying the poor, but identifying with them.

The focus demands changes in attitude and practices of governments, international institutions and the United Nations (UN), and also in personal lifestyles borne along on the supermarket culture and the use of money and power at the individual level. Advocacy, as the activated desire to influence key decision-makers in the world community, has become a natural extension of this approach. The Jubilee 2000 coalition, where the churches came together with others, showed how the empowerment of local people in strategic alliances has actually influenced G8 leaders, the World Bank and the International Monetary Fund (IMF). The reflection on biblical and theological themes also underlies the nature of Christian participation in social justice, human and environmental development issues. The World Bank and IMF have been criticised for pursuing market-led policies which are crushing the poor in many countries and expanding the gap between the poor and the rich.

Christian Aid Week: a case study

At a time when many agencies have abandoned house-to-house collections, Christian Aid Week in mid-May vivifies a typically Christian practice. Equipped with no less than 17 million of the famous red envelopes, an army of some 350,000 volunteer collectors takes to the streets of Britain and Ireland, and people give over £11 million in one week. It is a huge, well organised, Church-based outpouring of generosity, the prime impulse for which is that it is less about begging for money and more about 20,000-plus churches having an opportunity to respond directly to the Gospel. Or, as the donor or collector who has to go from door to door testifies, about 'sacrificial Christian giving'. For, the individual players are aware of the issues of international poverty and want to have an opportunity to respond. There is no evidence of compassion fatigue, rather the reverse. Emergency appeals have raised millions of pounds for Mozambique and then for Ethiopia even outside the Week.

Giving of time and money bears out Jesus' teaching that "where your money is, there your heart is also." Fuller commitment to poverty reduction tends to follow an initial donation, rather than commitment being a prerequisite for giving. The person who begins by putting money in the envelope often becomes a collector, then a representative, an organiser and a campaigner for justice. In recent years, the Week has also offered the resources to tackle the cause of poverty: for instance, the ironic fact that the poorest countries in the world pay millions of dollars every day to the richest. Even as Mozambique was being devastated by floods, it was paying over a million dollars a week to the richest countries and the richest financial institutions in the world. The sheer outrage of international debt has provoked Christian Aid Week supporters to tell the British government that these debts had to be cancelled. The then British prime minister Gordon Brown later said he received 100,000 postcards on the subject, adding ruefully 'and one of them was from my mother.' At the summit of rich country leaders that followed, commitments were made to cancel debt of $100 billion.

SIKHISM: BIRTH OF THE PURE

Sikhism, as a religion, originated in the Punjab in northwest India and has in recent years celebrated the tri-centenary of its formal institution. However, as a movement it was founded by the itinerant mystic Guru Nanak (1469-1539) who, in simplistic terms, sought to blend Hindu and Islamic elements in a single religious creed. The basically reformist and integrative content of this creed is aphoristically expressed in the motto he taught—"the unity of God, brotherhood of man, rejection of caste and the futility of idol worship." Nanak was followed by nine gurus, the last of whom, Guru Gobind Singh, founded the martial fraternity Khalsa (a word derived from Arabic, meaning "the pure") in 1699. The antagonistic relationship the Sikhs were set upon with the Delhi durbar of the Mughals, during Gobind Singh's time, was in many ways subliminally present in recent historical eruptions that problematised the community's unique position in the Indian nation.

It is beyond the brief of this chapter to rid an area of all the contradictions that are set up by the passage of an ideology of universality into that of a cult, a commune, a sect, or a modern religion with its own set of indentificatory cues and fixed boundaries. But a selective sketch of the historical context in which Sikhism was born—at the point of encounter of Hinduism and Islam, in the high noon of the Bhakti age—and the circumstances in which it evolved into its present form would help us parse this complex unit into its logical elements. Of course, Sikhism, like other religions, could be said to be still in evolution. New heretic streams and their standardisation or banishment, at one level, are signs of a natural movement to attain a measure of morphological complexity and the orthodoxy's equally natural attempt to limit such tendency. Another kind of border skirmish involves the bid to subsume Sikhism as a mere subset of a super-ordinate Hindu canvas and, hence, naturally, a more keenly-felt question of sovereignty.

The Sufi philosopher and saint Maulana Jalaluddin Rumi says in a Persian couplet: "The purpose of man's birth is to unite and not to divide". An eventful frontier of India, the site of many twists of history, was where a religion—envisaged like many others as a uniting factor for mankind—became embroiled in a set of political events of particularly sanguinary nature. Beyond all this, however, survives a basic guiding spirit of philanthropy in Sikhism with which we are directly concerned—a view that places the community at the centre of all thought and activity, and a cosmology that can be realised only through service to humanity. Perhaps the idea of seva, so essential to the Sikh way, cannot have been produced and honed to this degree of resonance without the often tumultuous, besieged life its adherents had to lead.

The Buddhist detour

For a true characterisation of Sikhism, one can't ignore its original liberatory intent and nature. The Manusmriti codified society into the chaturvarna the four varna ashramas, or castes but never intended to impose a regime of segregation by virtue of birth. The categories were meant to derive from occupation. But the priestly class misconstrued this philosophy, regulating society to suit its own interests. Around 2,500 years ago, when the Sudras received treatment no better than animals, the first stirrings of dissent were expressed via the personas of Mahavira and Buddha. Not being in conformity with the Brahminical credo, they became the object of a tide of counter-reaction. Jainism survived by transforming itself to be almost encompassed within the Hindu framework. Buddhism with its notion of universal brotherhood, revolt against the caste system, priestcraft and rituals met a more hostile fate. Monasteries, centres of power and affluence, were plundered; Brahmins infiltrated the sanghas; large-scale vandalism, massacre and destruction of stupas and idols took place. The impact of this militant campaign was absolute. Buddhism all but disappeared from India, the place of its birth.

It is possible to read the destruction of Hindu temples that began in the eleventh century as a reversal of the plot. Sultan Mahmud Ghaznavi's general, incidentally, was Buddhist. Low-caste Hindus too embraced Islam, forming another bulwark against caste Hindus. Buddhism as this kind of politicised religion saw its second coming in the twentieth century with Ambedkar's mass conversions. It is this moment Ambedkar's act of rejecting the religion of his birth—that places Sikhism, Islam, Christianity and Buddhism as neighbourly paradigms. He was in fact mulling over offers from the Muslims, Christians and Sikhs for the mass conversion of five million 'untouchables'. In 1936, Ambedkar even made public his intention to adopt Sikhism.

A series of discussions were held between the Sikhs, Ambedkar and RB Rajah apart from Dr Moonje, Savarkar, Malviya and JK Birla. The time and venue of the proposed ceremony were to be announced soon. It was aborted because of one factor: active and virulent opposition from Gandhi, who wrote to Dr Moonje on 31 July 1936 that it would subvert the spirit of the Poona Pact. He wrote a long article in *Harijan* on 22 August 1936, titled 'A Dangerous Proposal'. He said he could not countenance the *Harijan* going out of the Hindu fold. On 7 September 1936, he wrote to JK Birla, "today I will only say that to me Sikhism is a part of Hinduism". Further, "if you can make them give up the separate electorate (then existing in Punjab), then I will have no objection to Harijans calling themselves Sikhs".

Intrinsic philanthropism

What were the humanist aspects of Sikhism that attracted a statesman, philosopher and scholar like Ambedkar? It is presumed to guarantee a casteless society. In fact, it goes beyond to condemn the barrier between all religions. All paths to salvation are equal, and deserving of equal respect; no religion is superior. Simultaneously, it does not associate overtly with any of them. Its specificity lies in the fact that it is simultaneously a peace-loving, spiritual path and one that rebels against all oppression. Those conversant with Oriental thought fasten upon those passages in the Guru Granth Sahib which refer to thoughts of immanence and conclude that Sikhism is nothing but an echo of Hinduism. Those imbued with Mohammedan or Christian thought cite the transcendental passages and identify Sikhism with Islam or Christianity. Others, who know both, will see here a new, organic growth of thought.

The word Sikh is a Punjabi form of the Sanskrit word Shishya, meaning a learner or disciple. Guru Nanak—born 1469 in village Talwandi, later named Nankana Sahib, and now in Pakistan—visualised a society rinsed of all exploitation. Though Nanak was born in an upper-caste Khatri family, in adolescence itself he refused the thread ceremony. Espousing a spirituality borne by social concern, he did not confine himself to a life of prayer. His was an engaged spirituality. With his companions, the Hindu Bhai Bala and the rabab playing Muslim Bhai Mardana, he travelled widely to observe first hand various religious practices and to engage in dialogue. In India, he discoursed with the Yogis, Sidhs and Naths. He travelled to Tibet, Burma and Sri Lanka to dialogue with Buddhists. He went to Iran, Arabia and Iraq and met Muslim divines in Mecca and Baghdad. For 40 years, on four Udasis (travels), he travelled thousands of miles. Wherever he went, he proclaimed that there is but one God—One, formless, immortal, creator, sustainer and destroyer of all beings, pervading in his own creation. He sought to free worship from caste monopoly, to transfer religion from centres of scholasticism to common homes. He wanted men to love God without the aid of barren metaphysics, but via the selfless service of humanity.

It was a historically occasioned impulse that led Guru Gobind Singh to give the Sikh a final and complete shape. He baptised its adherents in the Sikh way, i.e., with amrit (nectar), to establish the order of Khalsa on the Baisakhi of 1699, at Anandpur Sahib. He made mandatory the five external symbols Kesh (unshorn, natural hair), Kangha (comb), Kachha (shorts, formerly a martial dress), Kada (iron bracelet) and Kirpan (sword). A person is not a Sikh automatically by birth, unless he or she is specially initiated into Sikhism as above. It is wrong to overstate here any deviation from Nanak's pacifism into a martial spirit. The first guru had, for the continuity and consolidation of his miraculous mission, not only declared the essential unity between him and his successor gurus (together spanning a period of 239 years from 1469 to 1708) but an identical spirit of dissent and rebellion was contained in their thoughts. Guru Gobind Singh, after completing the mission in consonance with the tradition of transfer of guruship to individuals, conferred the guruship after him to the Guru Granth and the Guru Panth, or the august body of the community collectively. Sikhism, thus, is not a set of views or doctrines, but a way of life lived according to a definite model of discipleship. The institution of guru is at all times operative in the career of the disciple, offering cohesion, direction and moral force to society.

Egalitarianism

India has for centuries treated people who live on bhiksha as revered, privileged well over those who work for the necessities of life. Being regarded as untouchables is the price for the sweat that flows in the service of society. In his travels, Nanak preferred to stay and dine with this class of people alone and declared, "Nanak is found among the lowest caste, what has he to do with the high and mighty? Wherever the lowliest are looked after, there lies the grace of Almighty God." He declared that, "he who earns livelihood with earnest labour and distributes it among fellow beings, can only know the path of Almighty God." His three basic commandments, in fact, are Naam Japo (remember God); Kirat Karo (do honest labour); Vand Chako (distribute among fellow beings). The last has now been qualified as Dasvandh i.e., distribution of one-tenth portion of the earning. Three institutions arose out of this egalitarianism. The Sarovar, or common bathing tank, a radical practice in days when water was a central tool in the idea of purity and pollution. The Sangat, a congregation without discrimination, and the Pangat, the common dining at the langar, were corollaries in this approach.

In 1571, Emperor Akbar wanted to call on Guru Amar Dass at Govindwal. He had first to take food in the Guru ka langar. On this occasion, Akbar offered the Guru a large estate for the maintenance of the langar. The Guru politely declined and said, "I have already obtained enough from the Creator. The people are my lands and estates. Enough that daily we get the bread from God. And that the Guru ka langar should be of the masses, by the masses and for the masses." As a token of his appreciation, Akbar presented it to Bibi Bhani, the Guru's daughter. Later, the Guru established a township on that land, the famous city of Amritsar. In 1598, Akbar came to see Guru Arjan Dev and had Guru ka langar. Again he offered a contribution. This Guru too declined, and said, "There is a severe famine in the country, and it would be best if thy imperial visit were to be marked by the remission of this year's land revenue to the farmers". Akbar gave orders accordingly. Equality is not exhibited in the langar alone, also in the battlefield. Once a Sikh, Bhai Kanehya Singh, was produced before Guru Gobind Singh with the complaint that he was offering water even to wounded enemy soldiers. His explanation that he could not distinguish between friend and foe pleased the Guru.

Women's equality
Renunciation and asceticism are not the ideal in Sikhism. It mandates a healthy involvement in the ordinary life of the householder, where men and women are tied in an equal partnership. Guru Nanak's conferment of an equal status to women was another of the meaningful, humane departures he made from the norm of the day. There is no separate code for women in Sikhism, they are on a par with men in all respects and can become priests and are empowered to administer amrit. Women have been as much partners in the battlefield as at the langar. Some practical steps also were made to ensure the equality of women. Prohibition of sati, purdah, dowry and female infanticide, and an allowance for widow remarriage can be counted among these.

Democracy
Traditionally, all Gurus have respected their Sikhs and listened to

their advice. Guru Ram Dass, the fourth guru, said: "There is no difference between Sikh and Guru, both are one and the same." Guru Gobind Singh, after administering amrit to the first Panj Pyaras, bowed before them to take amrit at their hands. Thus the Guru himself was baptised by his own baptised Sikhs, creating a history of equality between founder and disciples, and supremacy of the collective leadership over himself. As an analogous and widely known practice, anyone can be punished for breach of rules of conduct or for action contrary to the interest of the community. Even Guru Gobind Singh was once fined ₹125 for lowering his arrow in salute before the tomb of a saint, Dadu Shah, contravening the prohibition of grave worship, only to test his followers. Maharaja Ranjit Singh too was punished at the Akal Takht. In recent years, many political leaders and eminent members of the community were awarded similar punishment.

The martial form

In a seminal form, this might have been there since Nanak, who had seen the tyrannous aspects of the rule of Ibrahim Lodhi and Babar and was witness to the massacre at Eminabad, where he was imprisoned for revolt. There are enough verses to suggest he did not favour acquiescence. For example, "If you live even after your dignity is lost, it is sinful to have food." Or, "The king has become butcher and dharma has flown by wings." At another place, he said, "The rulers are tigers and the servants dogs, licking the blood of the common man." There is protest in these lines, expressed on behalf of the people and against the state, and perhaps it would be too easy to over-interpret them as anti-Delhi in some essential sense. As such, Guru Nanak was preparing the steel for the sword of the coming gurus, ploughing and sowing the seeds of revolution.

At any rate, the mutually accommodative compact between the gurus and the Mughal kings ended with the bloody takeover of Jehangir, who chased and killed his own son and rival Khusro, and ordered the execution of Guru Arjan Dev on the pretext of aiding the prince. The next guru, Hargobind Singh, established the Akal Takht as a temporal seat and resorted to weaponisation. He fought and won eight battles, but never acquired an inch of land. By deception, he was imprisoned for seven years in Gwalior and was released on the intervention of Muslim divines. The acrimony was complete when Guru Tegh Bahadur, the ninth guru, and his four grandchildren were put to death on the orders of Aurangzeb for refusing to convert. The rest is history.

Though political Islam and even political Hinduism have fought battles against the gurus, many devout Muslims and Hindus laid down their lives and sacrificed family and property for their sake. Proof that Sikhism was never against religion. Only against oppression would the Kirpan, the Merciful Sword, be ever raised in combat. The use of military power for the common weal is a phenomenon with some precedence in myth and history. A line connecting the Punjab and the rise of the Marathas comes with Sant Samrath Ram Dass, for whom a chance encounter with Guru Hargobind at Srinagar, Garhwal, in 1634 was a life-transforming experience. On his way back from Badrinath, he was stunned to see the pomp and show of the guru's retinue. He asked, "I had heard that you occupied the gaddi of Guru Nanak. Nanak was a tyagi sadhua saint who had renounced the world. You are wearing arms and keep an army and horses. You allow yourself to be addressed as Sache padshah, the true king. What sort of a sadhu are you?" The Guru replied, "Internally a hermit and externally a prince. Arms mean protection to the poor and destruction to the tyrant. Baba

Nanak had not renounced the world, only maya." This was the vision that was passed on to the Sant's disciple, Shivaji.

Poetry of the one

The Guru Granth Sahib is an anthology that stands as a unique social text which embodies the best of the Bhakti age. It contains the sacred poetic compositions of six Sikh gurus and 30 other Indian saints, and is a matchless treasure of wisdom, knowledge and experience of ascetics and seers—Muslim, Hindu, Sikh, and of all castes who lived, preached and practiced over a period of 500 years. The range of voices is stunning.

Hazrat Sheikh Farid (1175-1265) of Punjab, Sayyed Bhikhan and Bhai Mardana were Muslims. Ramanand of Banaras, Jaidev of Bengal (1201-1245) and Pannananda of Maharashtra were Brahmins. Kabir (1398-1495) was a weaver and Ravidas a shoemaker from Banaras, Trilochan a Vaish, Namdev an untouchable from Maharashtra, Sadna a butcher from Sindh and Bhagat Sain a barber. Guru Arjan Dev compiled it in five years, from 1599 to 1604, the only criterion being the concordance of a verse with the teachings of the Gurus. Gobind Singh added to it the compositions of Tegh Bahadur before bestowing guruship on the 1,430-page Gurmukhi text. The verses, in sadhu bhasha, other spoken languages from different parts of India and Persian and Sanskrit, are like streams come together in a universal reservoir of wisdom, humanism and grace.

Many of the verses exhibit a direct concern with doing good to others rather than empty, inward contemplation. Take this small sample. From Nanak: "He alone is the true human being, who receives good teachings and shows mercy to the living beings and gives something in charity." Guru Arjan Dev, in the widely read verses of Sukhmani Saheb, says: "False is the body which does not do any good to others." Kabir, the weaver-saint from Banaras, sang with his patented sublime irreverence, "When a man dies, he is of no use to any man, but when an animal dies, it serves ten purposes." And Parmananda, a Brahmin of Sholapur district of Maharashtra, says, "Oh Man! What is that you have attained by mere listening to the holy books? The spirit of worship of Lord is not cultivated in you. You have not helped any needy person." The release from a sacerdotal society to one where the love of God was within everyone's reach and was to be realised in an essential, radical humanism—that essence of the Bhakti philosophy is the foundation on which is built the edifice of the Sikh path.

At a more everyday level, Nanak sought to free people from disunity in forms of worship. Like the social organisation based on equality of human beings, he instituted a common mode of worship. Sangat was the initial name given to the place of mixed congregations where his disciples met in the mornings and evenings to sing hymns, perform seva, and derive inspiration to remould their lives. Later, the scope of activities of the Sangat expanded with night shelters and bathing facilities. It is in this concentrated vision of community life—where each is bound in a pact of duty towards the other, and where participatory service is at the centre of social obligations—that one can find the essential philanthropism of the Sikh way of life. Everyone is a potential beneficiary, and each is enjoined in a reciprocal set of obligations towards the community. This is the special philosophy that now governs the trajectory of several modern organisations working in the field of human rights, civil liberties, women's rights and many others. It mandates an active social order where there is no habitual, ritualistic charity.

Bhai Dayalchand Trust, New Delhi

Founded by an elderly Sikh, Bhai Veerji, who was a civil contractor who built many parts of the IIT Delhi Campus. He later realised at the Guru Tegh Bahadur Gurudwara that many of the poor and the homeless could not attend the Guru ka Langar (community feeding) which is famous in the Sikh community as their form of giving to society. He started the langar on a personal basis through his family trust Bhai Dayal Chand Trust. The whole family and now the extended family feed close to 10,000 people on Chandni Chowk streets, Nizamuddin and also other homeless people. Veerji is shy of publicity and doesn'tlike to be photographed. The efforts are completely localised. The food is donated by the community and cooked in Tilak Nagar (a suburb of Delhi) and brought to these areas by volunteers. This is a story of complete voluntary effort, unsung and unreported.

There are such efforts in every city in India but this goes on at religious centres on all days. However, most of them are registered as trusts and societies. The funding is localised and people contribute from their resources and are predominantly driven by religious philanthropy. They do not have full-time staff or an office. They usually operate from the home of the founder. This work will continue and provide succor to millions of people. During disasters such as the Gujarat earthquake, tsunami and cyclones, the Sikh Gurudwaras (temples) go in trucks to the affected location and feed people and provide relief irrespective of caste, religion or class. There are efforts by local people who do not want media attention and do their work quietly. Veerji the founder is no more but the work is carried on by the other members of his family who are inspired by the Sikh traditions and by their acts of giving.

CHAPTER 3

EVOLVING CIVIL SOCIETY IN INDIA—21ST CENTURY

We all have the same human body, the same human emotions and the same human mind. When you are aware of the fundamental truth of human existence as I do, others wish to overcome suffering, you automatically feel empathy and closeness for them. This is compassion. When you experience compassion for others, the first person to benefit is actually you. Compassion is a true source of happiness.

– His Holiness the Dalai Lama

The concept of personal philanthropy in India is part of one's religious activity, not a response to social needs. The major religions in India are based on a philosophy and cultural values for the individual soul, and doing good deeds is an important aspect of this.

The Indian context

Food is a major need and is given across castes. For example, a fresh chapati to a Brahmin widow, leftover chapati to the dog, oil or wheat flour to a passing Jogi (Bhargava caste), a chapati to the nearest cow and wheat husk or sugar for the ants. The principle is that God gives us enough so we can eat well and no one goes hungry from our door. At the 1986 Kumbh Mela, it was estimated that India has 8 million sadhus or yogis (saintly people). Many survive only by encouraging people's instinct to give. There are also hundreds of people of castes whose only role is to beg for food or take the clothes of the dead.

Mythology tells of Raja Harishchandra, who gave away everything to become a dom (someone who survives by cremating bodies). Even today in Gujarat, a rich diamond merchant or his son will become a Jain monk, throwing millions of diamonds to the public in a procession. Richard Lannoy tells us of the great merchant guilds that funded the Ajanta and Ellora complexes and supported large sanghas (groups) of Buddhist monks. Gandhi used this principle of community collection to support his ashrams. However small the donation, it connects each donor to an idea. The langar or the serving of food in most big gurudwaras is a metaphor for Guru Nanak's Kartarpur commune, where everyone worked together on the land and ate together. As well as giving money or food, people can give of themselves, their skills, their labour or shram daan, whether for community work such as cleaning tanks or for their ashram or guru. The best functioning religious institutions in India are the gurudwaras where Sikhs sweep and look after shoes—considered to be lower-class activities—and also cook for the langar.

In earlier societies it was not difficult to build a house using natural resources. Health was looked after by the local vaid, or traditional healer, and so philanthropy was mainly limited to food. A rich farmer once said the best remedy for sadness, depression, angst, vairagya or meaninglessness of life is to feed hundreds and thousands of people. Experiencing pure giving is supposed to help one feel catharsis. Indian non-governmental organisations (NGOs) need to make use of this major tradition of giving.

With Independence in 1947 came the rule of the state, the first Prime Minister Jawaharlal Nehru putting in place a mechanism for a welfare state. To a large number of the country's illiterate population this was merely a change of rulers from Britain to India's Congress party. Although the Prime Minister declared he was a servant of the people, the Indian political leadership generally did not recognise that they were not rulers but managers and custodians of the people. Perhaps the only person who brought back to focus fundamental Indian values, to the poor and underprivileged, was the Father of the Nation—Mahatma Gandhi. The NGO sector owes its origin to Gandhian principles and philosophy and practices. Community organisations, post-Independence, were village-oriented and often led and inspired by a charismatic individual. NGOs were founded by like-minded people attracted by this charismatic leader; as a team, they led, motivated and facilitated the community in addressing their needs and, most importantly, in giving voice to the unheard. NGOs thus emerged as organised, informal representatives of the people who could challenge and confront the establishment. They were therefore often seen as powerful organisations, capable of delivering services in an efficient and cost-effective manner. The negative side was that many people in government and in large businesses and industry regarded NGOs as troublemakers.

THE NGO SECTOR TODAY

Although it is difficult to provide precise statistics about the number and range of NGOs operating in India, they comprise a vast sector. The last estimate was 3.1 million NGOs by the Ministry of Statistics and Programme Implementation. This survey is flawed as it has enumerated all kinds of non-profits including clubs, sports associations and all registered under the Societies Registration Act and as Trusts. There is no area of human endeavour in which NGOs do not operate. At a local level, hundreds of thousands of self-help groups, youth associations, women's organisations and neighbourhood groups operate in both rural and urban areas. These are essentially informal NGOs, based on local inter-family, inter-household relationships addressing issues arising out of daily existence in those localities. Some of them have grown into larger associations with a membership base for example, forest workers' associations and tribals' associations as well as federations of residents associations.

Many religious organisations work in the social welfare and social development arena, either directly under the church, temple, mosque and gurudwara or through their extension programmes and departments. A vast number of educational institutions, primary schools, secondary and post-secondary colleges, vocational educational institutions and professional educational bodies also operate in the NGO sector. They provide employment to millions and are major providers of education, particularly in urban areas. Likewise, many health institutions, especially hospitals, are run as NGOs. These charitable hospitals range from small clinics in suburban areas and small towns, to large, sophisticated health facilities in metros.

Another broad area of activity is found in workers' organisations. Trades unions have a long tradition in India, going back to the nineteenth century. Massive organisations of workers exist in the urban industrial sector, in the office and government sector and also in many rural parts of the country (among agricultural and forestry workers and in the fishing, plantation and construction industries). Although trade unions are incorporated as independent NGOs, post-Independence India has seen a much closer relationship with political parties, which has undermined their autonomy.

The rise in professional associations in India has paralleled the developments in the late nineteenth century. Associations of artists, writers, etc., began more than a hundred years ago. In recent years, teachers, doctors, dentists, lawyers, engineers, managers, scientists, social workers, personnel managers all kinds of professionals have formed their own membership associations, which operate at local, provincial and national levels.

Many welfare organisations contributed to the welfare state. One of the most important contributions was that of the Leprosy Mission Trust. Its origin was in the Leprosy Mission established by the Anglican Church who also organised the Delhi Brotherhood society and the St Stephen's Society in Delhi. They began hospitals and community projects across India. On the outskirts of Delhi, a leprosy hospital was established in Shahdara. Leprosy patients cared for by the Leprosy Mission Trust and they had many projects across India. In India, there are an estimated million cases of leprosy. India's current leprosy prevalence rate (PR) is 0.72 per 10,000, though pockets of high endemicity still remain in the country.

Though India bears more than half the global leprosy burden, human rights issues associated with the disease are still not given due importance. The issues of people affected by leprosy taken up by National Human Rights Commission (NHRC) were more to do with benefits and entitlements. Inclusion of leprosy under the Prevention of Disability Act of 1995 was a starting point in claiming fundamental human rights.

Several provisions continue to discriminate against a person affected with leprosy. A few examples of such Acts considered discriminatory towards people affected by leprosy are the Indian Divorce Act 1869, Indian Christian Marriage Act 1872, Bombay Municipal Corporation Act 1888 and Dissolution of Muslim Marriage Act 1939. A few laws have been repealed by successful lobbying with the government of India and for policy through campaigning. An amendment bill to juvenile justice was passed in August 2011. It puts an end to the practice of separating children with leprosy from other infants in children's homes. The 1988 Motor Vehicle Act has also recently been revoked enabling those living with leprosy to obtain driving licences.

Stigma, ostracism and violation of human rights continue to affect the lives of people affected by leprosy. Awareness and advocacy initiatives are crucial to facilitate inclusion of people affected by leprosy and other disabilities into the mainstream at par with others to live with dignity. Therefore, it is important that the Leprosy Mission Trust continues to work with people affected by leprosy and other disabilities to empower them and promote positive change relating to leprosy and other disabilities.

Today, due to the work of the Leprosy Mission Trust and many NGOs in India, the scourge of leprosy and its stigma is almost over. A major contribution of the NGO sector has been the eradication of leprosy.

HelpAge India, another NGO founded in the late 1970s, began its work in building old age homes. Beginning with a home on the outskirts of Delhi at Fatehpur Beri near Chattarpur, today thousands of homes are being supported by HelpAge India. It has brought significant changes in the field of ageing in India by way of the National Policy of Ageing and National Policy for Health of the Elderly. HelpAge India had realised early that the demographic revolution and rising life expectancy meant that many would live longer and need more care than ever. More children migrated and created for parents a "lonely nest syndrome", more painful than previous generations. The famous Indian joint family has finally broken. HelpAge India continues to talk to children in more than 3,000 schools on values and on parenting. Children are responsible for their parents. The Maintenance of Parents Bill 2007—that children are responsible for their parents—is the direct outcome of HelpAge India's efforts. It is now mandatory for children to look after their parents. The National Policy for Older Persons is an effort to make future programmes age-friendly.

HelpAge India works in 87 districts of India and treats 1.25 million elderly every year. In the course of its work, HelpAge India had also discovered that many senior citizens in the villages were not only concerned about their own rights, but were also concerned about the future of their grandchildren. Pensions for the poor continue to be a problem in villages. Recently, they have embarked on a large coalition with Aruna Roy, Mazdoor Kisan Shakti Sangathan (MKSS) and Baba Adhav and Hamal Panchayat to fight for pension rights, called the Pension Parishad. The struggle is now for universal pension for all older persons in India. As a collective voice of India's senior citizen population, HelpAge India would like to see modifications in both the social pension sector as well as health insurance sector in order to bring about social security for the elderly.

Banyan was an effort of two young women Vandana Gopakumar and Vaishnavi Jayakumar. Vaishnavi, a young MBA student, saw the plight of a young woman, half naked, battered and bruised, and homeless in front of their college. They tried to reach out to this person out of compassion which resulted in the formation of Banyan, an organisation that works on mental health issues. They started to work primarily with women suffering from mental illness and consequent stigma and exclusion. Slowly, Banyan began to work on changing the boundaries of perception.

The girls began their work after Vandana completed her medical and psychiatric social work and Vaishnavi dropped out of her MBA programme. They were only 22 then. Since then, they have rehabilitated thousands of mentally ill women and men into the normal community. More than that, they have been able to advocate and influence the Mental Health Act. They received support from industrialists in Chennai who supported them, like the Rane Group, Hindustan Motors and others who willingly contributed time and resources to Banyan. Sankar Narayanan, Banyan chairperson, especially spends time to raise resources for the organisation.

The work of NGOs like Banyan compelled the government into a review of the Mental Health Act. Consequently, a chapter on mental health was included in the Twelfth Five Year Plan.

Navdanya is an organisation founded by Vandana Shiva, a leading activist in the advocacy against genetically modified (GM) food. She began her career as a management researcher on agricultural policies. Navdanya, which means nine seeds, is a movement to protect the rights of farmers over genetic material. Navdanya has created more than a hundred seed banks and worked with women farmers to save seeds and go organic. The movement has spread to 19 states and Vandana Shiva is one of the foremost activists in India. She is an architect of the Beej Bachao Andolan a movement to save and protect seeds which has grown in its efforts to prevent the onslaught of genetically modified food and GM seeds. Navdanya believes GM food and seed threaten the biodiversity of India and the freedom of its farmers. It is due to Vandana Shiva's efforts that the government did not accept GM food, especially GM brinjal. However, lobbies are actively at work to promote the interests of seed companies and GM food. Vandana Shiva is a one woman army who has held back the combined onslaught of such companies.

Navdanya also sells organic food at select outlets to mobilise resources for their campaign.

Organisations for mobilising resources

The NGO sector in India consists largely of Indian organisations. There are also foreign NGOs, some of which may be receiving local support but are largely unfettered by the need to raise funds. These include the Ford, MacArthur and Rockefeller Foundations, Oxfam, ActionAid, Plan International, World Vision, Save the Children Fund, Population Council and Population Services International. There are also UN organisations, multilateral donor organisations and bilateral donor organisations. This section deals with indigenous Indian NGOs. The major hurdle for NGOs in accessing financial resources is credibility. Because most NGOs owe their existence to a charismatic leader, their success rate in mobilising financial resources depends on the credibility of that individual. Once an NGO has been able to demonstrate its capability and effectiveness, however, access to funds ceases to be a major problem. The critical years are those before the NGO has established a track record and then again when it has grown organisationally and reached a plateau. Accessing financial resources at this later stage becomes a real challenge. It is in this context that we now deal with specific areas.

FUNDING SOURCES FOR THE NGO SECTOR

Indian funding comes from four main groups: government, private foundations, business and individuals. Broadly speaking, the financial requirements of NGOs fall in two categories: operations administration overheads, salaries and wages, rentals, equipment, infrastructure, etc.; and programme-related direct costs involved in implementing the programme. With a few notable exceptions, most local funding sources do not support overhead or operational expenses. Unfortunately, the grants from government and of donor NGOs also do not fund overheads and infrastructure. Programme support is relatively easier to fund but an NGO has to ensure that the programme is in line with the donor's guidelines, philosophies and interests. As a result, most of the NGO sector is still heavily donor-dependent, and finds it extremely difficult to obtain resources for creating an endowment or corpus comprising only Indian funds. This reluctance by the state to support overheads and build corpus funds has made it necessary for NGOs to turn to international donors and foundations. It is rare to find a significantly large NGO that does not have international support. Before discussing current trends in local funding, it is worth noting the constraints on NGOs becoming financially sustainable and viable. The rules regulating the investment of endowment or corpus funds or even short-term programme funds are highly restrictive, with virtually no option to access international markets. Investments may be made only in government securities and approved mutual funds and in public sector organisations, which usually offer the lowest returns compared with blue chip and gilt-edged investment in private institutions and organisations. NGOs cannot access the capital market other than in the form of bonds and instruments issued by the government or its agencies. NGOs may not invest in shares, under current laws. The regulations in India reflect the government's understanding and perception of the role of NGOs. The government seems to find it impossible to regard an NGO as a group of highly motivated, dedicated people with a missionary zeal to do good, without compensation, and functioning out of accommodation with obvious costs as rent, electricity, telephone and computer. Clearly, paper for correspondence may be obtained free and handwritten with pens, also obtained free, and delivered personally on foot, as postage is not recognised as a cost by the government. Through individual donations, subscriptions and often personal interest, NGOs, largely at the initiative of a charismatic leader, have been able to generate resources to provide for overheads. But the problem of building a corpus or endowment remains.

Government, central and state

The government is the largest single source of funding for NGOs. Funds are administered and budgeted by a ministry, as a resource for development. The amounts may vary, depending on the allocation and the ministry's basic responsibility. The rules and procedures also vary greatly, and in most cases are complex and lacking in clarity causing major problems for NGOs trying to access funds from a government ministry or department. There is no directory that lists schemes supported by each ministry. Some ministries have attempted such a listing but most are not easily accessible to NGOs. A few ministries have guidelines for funding applications but their format is not user-friendly. Following up a proposal for approval by government is perhaps the most nonproductive and time-consuming activity of an NGO until the initial grant is received. Procedural and bureaucratic formalities delay the release of subsequent installments and NGOs often have to raise bribing support (graft to move the bureaucratic process) pending the receipt of the next installment. It becomes imperative for all NGOs accessing initial government funding to come to an administrative arrangement on this.

Private foundations

A list of all funding units or foundations and trusts, giving details of areas of interest, guidelines for grants, etc., is available from Sampradaan Indian Centre for Philanthropy (ICP), New Delhi. As with individual giving, local companies that set up their own private foundations initially focused mainly on religious institutions, temples, dharmashalas, animal shelters and pilgrim facilities, closely followed by support for educational institutions. Support to health-related organisations was a distant third. There are no figures of the amount involved but, generally speaking, it would seem to be about $200 million (₹8 billion) (Source: Dimensions of the Voluntary Sector, a CAF-VANI publication).

Corporate giving

Because the Indian corporate sector is emerging as a serious player in philanthropy, this category is dealt with in some detail. Most corporate giving is at the initiative of an individual—usually the chief executive or his immediate family members. Such support has not yet become part of corporate policy and largely depends on the discretion of the individual. Azim Premji of Wipro decided to give away a large portion of his wealth to Azim Premji Foundation and dedicated a substantial portion to primary education in India, particularly Karnataka where he hails from. This has inspired others in Bangalore who made large fortunes from the information technology revolution and the long tax holiday offered by the government. Azim Premji Foundation is like the Bill and Melinda Gates Foundation of India.

Nevertheless, a significant change has taken place with the liberalisation and globalisation of the Indian economy. The emergence of joint ventures (JVs) of Indian companies with large international corporations is of significance. Indeed, the Indian partner is influencing in no small measure its JV partner, through strong involvement in social development, corporate philanthropy and corporate social responsibility.

There are also a few good experiments in development being funded by corporate trusts. Notable among them are Arvind Mills, Tatas and Lupin Laboratories, as well as many others operating in their states of origin. There are large hospitals functioning in Gujarat, Rajasthan and Maharashtra, funded by business families of Mumbai who make annual visits to their havelis in rural areas. Particularly in Gujarat, there is a strong culture of funding both locally and from non-resident Indians. These resources are made available to all kinds of community efforts in health, education, technology, watershed management and improvements for the tribals. A study of Gujarati philanthropy would require a whole thesis. It looks beyond caste and at the Gujarat state as a whole. More money would be raised if fundraising was made a little more area or region-specific, or connected to recognisable affected regions. Funds from New Delhi and Mumbai could be directed to poor areas in Uttar Pradesh, Bihar and Odisha, where the labour comes from. In Bangalore, the money collected could fund North Karnataka or Tamil Nadu's poorer regions. In Bangalore, Titan Watches has started contributing to organisations working in the field of disability. It works with Myrada, a Bangalore-based NGO working with women's groups, which has begun manufacturing watch straps for Titan.

Corporate sponsorship

A number of private and public sector companies will support voluntary agencies but they usually have specific areas of interest and most want to get mileage out of giving. The main areas are for caring benefits. Many large industrial houses have their own foundations and do not give to other agencies.

A notable example in the past decade has been ICICI Bank supporting initiatives in primary education. It also helped an NGO, Pratham, in Mumbai. Citibank has sponsored four NGOs through Charities Aid Foundation microcredit grants amounting to about $100,000 (₹4 million): Sharan in Delhi, Sarba Shanti Ayog in Kolkata, Working Women's Forum in Chennai and SPARC (Society for the Promotion of Area Resource Centres) in Mumbai.

Individual and community giving

A dilemma for Indian NGOs is how much local funding (Swadeshi) to access, and how much foreign funding (Videshi). An associated question is how to make individuals and their communities feel the need to give more, not through the state but through a voluntary system. Not by civil legal pressure but by moral pressure. To achieve this, the accepting agency must be more credible, less self-serving, more humane and sensitive, and less bureaucratic. People expect purity, transparency and simplicity of operation, so the desire to give can easily be snuffed out by even small examples of waste or corruption in the NGO sector. Even when giving to God there is an expectation of return. Only highly effective gods or goddesses get funds while millions of religious places lie in neglect. The need to give is usually directly proportional to the person's luck or success in receiving material rewards. People who give also want to see visible results of giving. Such results are easy to show in terms of medicines given, sick people treated, students educated, trees planted or orphans looked after. It is difficult to get funds for gender awareness, health research, mental illnesses, and development and income generation activities that need long-term vision. People never tire of giving to God, because God is seen as perpetually giving to them as individuals. But they tend to tire of giving to causes that are like 'black holes of universal suffering'. Programmes have to be seen to support, to empower or to create self-reliance. Many people in rural areas contribute in kind, such as rice, wheat, and sometimes cows and other food items.

How does one apply funding to a community's needs and to compassion as a sustainable social programme? Who can be the agency is it individuals who inspire trust, institutional NGOs, voluntary groups, or all of them together? What roads would we take in the Indian context? At the end of this chapter we look at four case studies of indigenous fundraising in India. Each case study raises its own questions for the wider applicability or success of collecting community support in terms of skill, time and funds.

The act of giving when one wants to, is different from being pressed or reminded repeatedly to give. The latter takes away the free-choice element of giving and starts to feel like a tax. For example, the Rashtriya Swayamsevak Sangh (RSS), a volunteer Hindu right wing organisation involved in mobilising political support for the Bharatiya Janata Party (BJP), celebrates a teacher respect day in which people leave money in a daan patra (donation box) and no one knows how much anyone has given. Many donors do not want tax receipts, because they do not want anyone to judge the size of their donation. Only the rich who sponsor a building or a fan or a bench are named. Every step on the climb to Vaishno Devi, a Hindu shrine, has a name carved on it, but this is a Hindu practice not seen in the Sikh or Islamic faiths.

The reasons to go Swadeshi are clear. About 80 per cent of NGO funding is foreign, and can be culturally and politically suspect because there is less accountability to India's authorities. In Bangladesh, for example, foreign funding can be cut off by any political party that feels antipathy to the liberal Left, Christian or Islamic basis of funding.

Products and services

Many NGOs have seen that traditional sources of grants or donations—whether from institutions or from individuals—tend to specify their end use, and few give the NGO sufficient freedom to use them the way the NGO wishes. However, donations of products and services can generate business-like resources for the NGO.

Kolkata-based Silence and Delhi-based Amar Jyoti produce various products of extremely good quality that are then sold. Silence works with hearing-impaired people, and exports products to European countries. It also provides computer-based data entry services to several corporate houses in Kolkata.

Karm Marg, a small NGO in Delhi, works with streetchildren. It collects waste paper and various other articles from companies and recycles them to sell as envelopes, paper bags, and so on. Another agency modelled on the same lines called Goonj collects old clothes and bric-a-brac and sells them to provide funds to other agencies. Sometimes old clothes are also transported to needy areas.

Agencies such as the Child in Need Institute (CINI) in Kolkata and the Comprehensive Health Development Programme (CHDP) at Pachod in Aurangabad sell health training services to various organisations, including government functionaries. Similarly, Eklavya runs courses for teachers in primary schools on a fee basis; and the Society for Participatory Research in Asia (PRIA) in Delhi runs management and other courses in participatory learning for several NGOs.

Reaching the Unreached (RTU) in Madurai and the Pan Himalayan Grassroots Organisation in Ranikhet offer construction and carpentry services to companies and individuals on a fee basis. The Habitat Technology group in Thiruvananthapuram has a large income from low-cost homes and buildings.

Sanchar, a communications group in Dehra Dun, performs plays and designs communications kits for several NGOs. It is now called the Mountain Children Forum.

Several NGOs such as the Ecumenical Christian Centre (ECC) in Whitefield, Seva Mandir (Rajasthan) and Chetna (Ahmedabad) lease their conference centre and training centre, the income going to the organisation.

Volunteers for projects

India has always had a tradition of volunteering although stronger in some periods than in others. A supreme example of volunteerism would be India's struggle for Independence, in which millions participated. Many religions require each person to do community work.

Voluntary contributions of labour (shram daan) have been common in many projects run by NGOs. This considerable contribution has rarely been measured by donor agencies or by the voluntary agencies themselves. The Charities Aid Foundation

(CAF) estimates that, if the value of this work were calculated at minimum wage rates, it would be in the region of ₹300 million.

Formal volunteering is now encouraged in schools and universities. Some NGOs have been targeting the youth in Delhi to persuade them to volunteer with certain projects:

- Pravah encourages students in schools and colleges to give their time to select NGOs. Pravah has a good network among school teachers. Pravah was started by Ashraf Patel, a young management graduate.

- Youth Reach encourages young corporate executives to volunteer time and also sponsors some of their executives to work with NGOs. Youth Reach was started by Uday Khemka, son of a famous industrialist involved with the Khemka Foundation.

- HelpAge India encourages senior citizens to volunteer in their programmes; some of their staff is also retired people. This group is growing and is actively beyond 20,000 volunteers. HelpAge India also works with 3,000 school volunteers who spend summer holidays in community service.

- Sruti encourages rural activists and volunteers who work in tribal areas and also support them to form community-based organisations. They have worked for 25 years and many of them are called Sruti fellows. Sruti was started by a young activist Kanika Satyanand who encouraged these activists and also raised finances. Sruti raises funds in innovative ways to fund Sruti fellows.

Resources through membership fees

There are many network agencies in India but membership fees usually comprise a small portion of their resources. In Mizoram, however, is an agency called Central Young Mizo Association; its work is supported entirely by membership fees of its 300,000 volunteer members. They have planted 600,000 hectares with trees and were awarded the Indira Gandhi Vrikshamitra Award for Environmental Excellence.

Resources through investments and securities

This kind of investment is limited, though agencies that have large corpus funds make investments and use the interest to cover operational costs. However, NGO funds can be invested only in government securities and safe instruments so the yield is low.

Non-resident Indians and the Indian diaspora

Some US-based foundations such as Aid to India's Development (www.aidindia.org) and Asha for Education (www.ashanet.org) support Indian projects with funding mostly from Indians living in the US. There are also millionaire Indians in the US who have set up a foundation, a famous one being The Indus Enterprise (TIE) headed by Kanwal Rekhi. An organisation called IPAN—India Partners Network run by Abhay Bhushan helps Indian NGOs raise funds in the United States.

In Singapore, Jayesh Parekh, who is part owner of Sony Broadcasting Television, has set up a pro-poor website (www.propoor.org) that focuses on the South Asian voluntary sector. Some Indian charities have set up charitable not-for-profit companies registered in the US; for example, CRY (Child Relief and You) and TERI (Tata Energy Research Institute) have formed Friends of CRY and Friends of TERI.

Foreign sources of funds

Grants made by foreign countries in 2010 and 2012 averaged ₹23 billion, while every year the total saving to the Indian economy was ₹281 billion … and this is only the official figure. Not included in this is much of the 500 tonnes of gold valued at ₹200 billion and at least 25 per cent of the black economy. Even 1 per cent of this saving is ₹2.81 billion, and if we include 1 per cent of the savings of non-resident Indians, which amount to about $1 billion (₹38 billion) a year, we are looking at over ₹30 billion that could be targeted for funding. If the amounts currently locked in millions of private charitable trusts (Hindu, Sikh, Wakf board and company trusts) and in large black economy transactions could be released, a huge amount of money would become available to the compassion sector. Some years ago, the nations in the industrialised West decided that they would transfer 0.7 per cent of their GDP to societies in developing countries as grants. Only Sweden has achieved that figure, the average amount being about 0.2 per cent. India's GDP in 1996-97 was ₹1,119.913 billion; 0.7 per cent of this is ₹78.39 billion, which is equivalent to federal government spending on education, health, housing, water, labour welfare and social welfare. Even half of this 0.35 per cent would be triple the total amount of foreign funding (₹39 billion). By 2010 it had come to as low as 0.1 per cent of the GDP.

Foundations and grant-making organisations

Most international funding agencies have one thing in common: they see themselves not as mere donors but as resource agencies and partners in the process of development. Their focus and programme priorities may vary but they view funding as a time-limited intervention that can ultimately lead to self-sufficient projects.

They all work through partner agencies, having close interaction with the agencies assisted. With few exceptions, the association is one of mutual respect and cooperation.

One of the major requirements for the successful and effective functioning of an NGO is adequate finance and its proper management. Although this concept of financial self-sufficiency for an NGO has been acknowledged both by the funding agencies and by the NGOs, the reality is different. Whilst some NGOs have an adequate financial base and manage their resources imaginatively, most of them do not, which adversely affects their efforts to achieve development objectives.

The reasons for this unsatisfactory situation are two-fold. First, NGOs generally depend on donations and grants from external and domestic agencies and individuals. Unfortunately, these agencies focus primarily on projects when making donations or grants. The money is given for a specific short-term project and the funding agency limits its interest in the NGO to the successful completion of the project it has approved. Its interest in the NGO ceases with the conclusion of the project and receipt of the NGOs report. In other words, the funding agency is interested in the activities of the NGO rather than the organisation itself. The institutional development of the NGO is of low priority for funding agencies, and NGOs are seldom given assistance for capacity development to initiate and manage large-scale programmes and development initiatives.

The second reason is that NGOs spend considerable time, energy and resources in preparing fundraising proposals, negotiating with donors and keeping separate accounts involving elaborate procedures. All these factors have a discouraging effect on NGO efforts to create the capital resources they need to achieve financial independence. Only a change from the project-oriented approach to long-term flexible institutional development will enable NGOs to become financially self-sufficient.

NGOs, too, must look at their policies if they are to become financially autonomous. The view prevalent among NGOs that their existence and growth depend totally on donations and grants, should give way to new concepts in achieving self-sufficiency. They must develop an element of enterprise, perhaps growing into organisations that provide goods and services that can be sold at realistic prices. This does not mean that NGOs should become businesses governed by profit. But such an attitude would encourage them to have a long-term plan for their programmes and to work towards a self-financing strategy that includes issues such as interest from investments and the sale of products and services. Financial self-sufficiency and effective financial management are crucial if NGOs are to make a meaningful and sustained contribution to society. This will be possible only if, on the one hand, donor agencies change their approach to funding and, on the other, NGOs change their attitude.

Several international charities and foundations have offices in India. Notable among them are Action Aid, the Aga Khan Foundation, the Christian Children Fund, the Ford Foundation, Friedrich Ebert Stiftung, Oxfam (UK), Plan International, Save the Children Fund and World Vision. Many of them have Indianised and have reduced funding to Indian NGOs.

FUTURE OF FUNDING TO CIVIL SOCIETY

Funding to India will slow down due to recession in the US and Europe. Foreign funds, according to home ministry sources (FCRA department), have reached a plateau in the past three years at ₹10,000 crore to about 30,000 organisations. Local resources have increased and the growing middle-class has also started to give. The role of Swadeshi funding is rising and more private foundations have been registered by new millionaires. There are several such foundations in the information technology city of Bangalore and also corporate foundations in other parts. The future will be driven within India and not from foreign aid. All international organisations are also registering in India to get a share of the pie. However, the future will depend on the value civil society delivers and not by social messages alone.

Foreign funding will decline and is already less than 0.1 per cent of the GDP. Corporate funding under the new Companies Act, Section 134 and 135 will bring close to ₹0.25 billion to the sector. The government has mandated that 2 per cent of profits before tax should be devoted to corporate social responsibility (CSR) programmes.

Fundraising as a professional activity

Resource mobilisation in India will become a highly professional activity in the next five to ten years. The focus will be on individuals and the private (business) sector, as well as the state and federal governments; the proportion of foreign aid will shrink. Although money will always be needed, the emphasis will be on tapping other resources. Mobilising human talent people with knowhow will become an in thing: many people are willing to share their expertise with NGOs during their vacations and weekends. Moreover, many companies are willing to give their executives time off for a good cause. The experience of the past few years has shown that there is considerable potential for fundraising to support programmes.

There are institutions with resources looking for worthwhile programmes and competent NGOs. There are individuals and business organisations willing to support good causes. Generally, there is increasing recognition among the growing middle-class that they have an obligation to provide for the less fortunate. Most of these individuals and organisations cannot reach the genuine beneficiary direct; they need the support of NGOs to translate their latent urge into tangible work. India and its 300 million middle-class can contribute a lot to transform Indian society. The potential giving in India is upwards of ₹16 billion (Source: A Sampradaan study).

South Asian Fundraising Group, New Delhi

South Asian Fundraising Group (SAFRG) was born in 1987 to train Indian NGOs in fundraising. HelpAge India and CRY which began in 1978, established that Indians were willing to give for the elderly and for children. They showed the way and were quickly followed by Concern India in Mumbai and SOS Children Villages in Delhi. HelpAge India was instrumental in setting up SAFRG in India. It was established to achieve, inter alia, the following objectives:

- Highlight the importance of self-reliance by fundraising among voluntary agencies;
- Provide a forum for exchange of ideas and to share fundraising experiences;
- Conduct and encourage research relating to the development of the concept of fundraising;
- Facilitate NGOs to embark on public fundraising in an ethical and professional manner.

Centre for Advancement of Philanthrophy, Mumbai

The Centre for Advancement of Philanthrophy (CAP) was founded by VM Lala of the Tatas who also looked after the Sir Dorabji Tata Trust. He established CAP and placed Noshir H Dadrawala as its head. Mentored by the late HD Parekh of HDFC, CAP today occupies a niche as a support organisation for incorporated charities, including grant-making trusts and foundations, NGOs engaged in development work and NGOs providing support to other NGOs. It has remained focused on legal and regulatory matters pertaining to incorporation, taxation, accounting and statutory reporting.

CAP is not a funding organisation although it conducts useful and informative workshops and training to help organisations improve their fundraising. CAP has also published a useful resource book on the subject, the *The Art of Successful Fundraising*.

They do not undertake registration but merely guide and assist organisations and individuals. CAP also guides and assists corporates with their CSR (Corporate Social Responsibility) initiatives, often helping them find credible NGO partners or guiding them with due diligence issues. CAP has also helped companies like Titan, Thermax, Forbes Marshal, Zensar, Atlas Copco, etc., set up their own corporate foundations.

Bhagwan Mahaveer Viklang Sahayata Samiti, Jaipur

The Bhagwan Mahaveer Viklang Sahayata Samiti (BMVSS) was set up in 1975 in Jaipur by Padma Bhushan Devendra Raj Mehta to provide artificial limbs with a focus on the poor. Mehta, now the Chief Patron, decided to set up the BMVSS after he met with a life-threatening road accident that crushed one of his legs with doctors fearing that it might have to be amputated. His life and limb were saved and Mehta went on to bring succour to many accident victims.

The Jaipur Foot was designed by Ram Chander Sharma under guidance of Dr Pramod Karan Sethi, then head of Orthopaedics at Sawai Mansingh Medical College in Jaipur, for which Sethi received the Magsaysay Award for Community Leadership in 1981.

The Jaipur Foot costs about $50 (about ₹3,000), while an imported artificial limb could cost well upwards of $2,000 (above ₹19,000). The BMVSS fits the prosthetic device free of cost. The Jaipur Foot has also become popular in Africa and Latin America because of its utilitarian design and low cost. It is India's non-profit export to other countries.

Understanding potential donors and resource institutions will involve studying their needs and expectations and designing schemes or work programmes that provide them with an opportunity to identify with a good cause. In short, NGOs should reach them at the right time with the right message. An NGO must be able to communicate well and regularly with potential donors. The fundraiser must believe totally in the cause and be confident.

The job of fundraising is not really about getting money. It comes as a result of a shift in people's thinking regarding money. The fundraiser, then, must shift the way people relate to it. They will say there is no money, that people cannot be trusted with their money, their money will not make a difference, and so on. The task of the fundraiser is to change this thinking and persuade them to express their commitment to the cause or programme. Contributing money then becomes just one form of their expression of commitment. The fundraiser must create a relationship with the contributor and provide opportunities to contribute again. It is important to report back to contributors, telling them how their money is helping to improve lives.

Chapter 4

CURRENT STATE OF
CIVIL SOCIETY WORK

"NGOs are leading and governments are devising responses to protect the most vulnerable populations: women, children, women , elderly and the poor from the impacts of the various crises. Connecting all these groups working on these same interlinked crises can achieve their shared vision of 'The World as We Want It to Be'."

– Hazel Henderson

There are a variety of non-governmental organisations (NGOs) working in India today, from those organised for immediate relief and charity to those that fight entrenched interests. Delivery system NGOs are the greatest in number, and aim to offer more effective and sensitive development and social services than the government. NGOs generally function in a two-tier system consisting of an apex level for investigative research and a second, district, level where they develop an affinity with the local people with whom they intend to work. The larger NGOs have independent sources of funding;

the others may have to be funded by government, provision for funding being built into each project.

The NGO delivery system has several weaknesses, including:

- smallness of scale and extremely talent-intensive organisations, which limits the replicability of their models;
- centralised decision-making, often being dependent on a charismatic leader;
- uncertainty about the continuity of schemes that depend on the availability of funds.

Despite these shortcomings, the strengths of the NGO delivery system are increasingly being appreciated by policymakers in the government. The NGOs have a higher level of motivation and dedication, as well as creativity and innovation, than government officials. They have far greater face-to-face interaction with local people, they are more responsive to people's aspirations and more sensitive to equity and gender issues. Their sanctions are based on consensus and social pressure rather than on coercion backed by state authority. They have greater organisational flexibility and generally follow a more holistic approach than the sectoral departmental character of government systems.

In the 1990s, there was a rise of several governmental programmes in which NGOs were assigned an important role. The best examples of these programmes, in which both government and NGOs act as facilitators, are: the mass campaign for literacy; the Women's Development Programme, popularly known as the Saathin's programme of Rajasthan; and Joint Forest Management. The major difference in these programmes from the past has been their focus on empowerment through mass mobilisation, motivation and organisation, with information on rights, laws and schemes, and through training. Because the philosophy of empowerment runs counter to the established image of government as a coercive institution, such programmes are not well understood by the bureaucracy, especially at the lower levels.

The relationship between the NGOs and the bureaucracy in India is a complex one, characterised by mutual suspicion and hostility. While the NGOs regard the bureaucracy as inherently insensitive, oppressive, inefficient, parasitic and corrupt, the image of NGOs among government officers is that of troublemakers and wasters, who are totally dependent on foreign funding. The fact that most NGO staff today, unlike their predecessors 20 years ago, no longer have an austere lifestyle and are well-paid professionals opting for social work as a mainstream (and frequently international) career adds to such an impression. The conflict between the two is often due to misunderstanding and confusion about each other's role. To illustrate, we consider the role of NGOs in the forestry sector.

NGOs and the forest department

As in similar other interventions, the role of NGOs in community forestry and joint forest management has been a hotly debated issue. Some feel that it is unnecessary to involve NGOs, except in certain problem areas. Others contend that they have a major role to play, albeit a complementary one. The anti-NGO group feels that the reorientation of the Forest Department could be achieved without the help of NGOs. Informal village committees for forest protection have to function effectively on their own because most villages in the country do not have viable NGOs.

The proponents of NGOs believe that their role is complementary to that of forest protection committees (FPCs). Their most important objective is to build the capability of village institutions to manage common property resources, a task that is highly intensive and requires interaction with villagers over a long period. In addition, the NGOs can disseminate information, act as a channel of communication between the Forest Department and the people, provide training and technical input, and resolve conflicts. They do not intend to usurp the role played by FPCs. Many conflicts between the NGOs and the Forest Department are due to the ownership problem, in which both become over possessive of their adopted villages or FPCs and see the other as potential threat to their influence and authority in the village. Described below are two incidents: in one the NGO sought but was not given active help from the Forest Department because the Department considered that local problems should be solved by the NGOs themselves; in the other, the Forest Department considered the attitude of the NGO patronising.

Seva Mandir, a large and well-regarded NGO, was working in village Shyampura (Rajasthan) for over a decade in adult education and irrigation. In 1985, the Forest Department planted trees on half the Department land pertinent to the village. Seva Mandir decided to plant trees on the other half, but ran into problems. After giving the NGO permission, the Forest Department withdrew from the picture; without the Department's help the NGO was unsuccessful in removing encroachments or in solving the problem of illegal grazing of cattle belonging to a neighbouring village. The possibility of employment attracted people initially, but after two years the project had not generated enough grass or NTFPs (non-timber forest products) to sustain people's interest.

In March 1993, the Vikram Sarabhai Centre for Development Interaction (VIKSAT), Ahmedabad, working in Gujarat, complained to the Divisional Forest Officer (DFO). The NGO maintained that the way the Forest Department worked in the village did not enhance the capability of the village society, as their members were not being involved in the decisions, and that the villagers were not happy with the manner in which benefits were distributed. The DFO sent a copy to the village for comments. The letter was considered by the executive council of the FPC in April 1993, and it entirely disagreed with the allegations of the NGO. The executive council threatened to take the NGO to court if the 'wild allegations' were not withdrawn. They also indicated that they did not need help from the NGO in future. The NGO explained that it wanted to enhance the capability of the village society so that it would become independent. This incident, however, led the NGO to withdraw from helping village development directly, and it decided to concentrate on training for other societies at its head office. VIKSAT was set up by Vikram Sarabhai's son Kartikeya Sarabhai to create awareness on environment using scientific techniques in Ahmedabad. It later led to the formation of the Centre for Environmental Education (CEE), Ahmedabad which has pioneered training in thousands of schools on environmental awareness.

New challenges

Government-sponsored development programmes and NGO-initiated activities currently operate in different spheres with little or no flexibility for coordination, often reinventing the wheel and duplicating each other's efforts. NGOs are reluctant to participate in government programmes because of their suspicion that the bureaucrats might have a hidden agenda (control), while positive bureaucratic changes conducive to NGO involvement that happen at higher levels affect only the most senior officials in the government. A major challenge will be to achieve bureaucratic reorientation, including a change from authoritarian to participatory styles and a shift in responsiveness from orders from above to demands from below.

Although voluntary action in India is growing and gaining significance in influencing national development, there is rising concern among the international donor agencies, governments and even NGOs themselves that the institutional capacity of NGOs needs to be strengthened if they are to become effective development agents. For instance, NGOs engaged in addressing environmental concerns are faced with multiple challenges. At one level are technical challenges such as those in community forestry, where there is a need to procure good quality seeds, select proper nursery sites, transport and plant seedlings, protect and manage the trees, and ensure the equitable distribution of benefits through community-based arrangements. At organisational levels there are difficulties in conducting proper needs assessments, recruiting and training staff, maintaining trainers' skills through refresher training courses, establishing sound fundraising strategies, mobilising local in-kind contributions from economically disadvantaged communities, resolving conflicts in their organisational structure, maintaining relationships with government departments and other voluntary resource organisations, complying with the administrative and programme requirements of donor agencies, and dealing with political pressures, all without losing independence and integrity.

Thus, major effort is required to promote the importance of institutional development among governments, donors and NGOs, to explain the basic concepts and strategies and, finally, to train people in carrying out institutional development.

Another problem in the non-governmental sector today is the rapid growth in number and wide dispersal of NGOs over the past decade. In trying to respond to a plethora of needs and funding opportunities, NGOs sometimes become good at nothing other than packaging proposals for donors. Furthermore, competition for funds, professional jealousy, differences in operational traditions and the desire to serve donors better are common maladies that restrict inter-NGO collaboration. A study by Professional Assistance for Development Action (PRADAN), a New Delhi-based voluntary research organisation (VRO), indicates that NGO effectiveness and the opportunities for their organisational development are hampered because they are isolated in rural areas.

Government support for NGOs

Although the concept of voluntary work is not new to India, the issue of cooperation and partnership between government and the NGOs was formally accepted only in 1985, in the federal government's seventh Five Year Plan. This acknowledged the important role that NGOs could play in the country's socio-economic development, which until then was considered to be the sole preserve of the public sector. The Plan recognised for the first time that the lack of success of the previous four decades of programmes sponsored and implemented by government had been for want of the people's participation; the new agenda offered by NGOs looked promising because, as well as being people-centered, it claimed to be innovative and cost-effective.

It was admitted that the NGOs, with their knowledge of the cultural and socio-economic conditions of the local population, coupled with a great deal of organisational flexibility and highly motivated staff, are more effective than governments in promoting social change at the grassroots level. In many cases, NGOs can visualise the interdependence between the different sectors, such as forestry, agriculture and health, and integrate them appropriately into their programmes.

NGOs have advantages over most public hierarchies; for example, in the tasks of reaching, informing, educating and mobilising the poor in inaccessible areas. As organisations driven by social values such as self-reliance and self-governance, NGOs can identify with the interests of the poor, and their high degree of commitment makes them well suited for initiating grassroots action. With a role in advocacy, NGOs are able to demand public accountability, effective popular participation in the process of decision-making at all levels and recognition of the legitimacy of dissent.

An NGO can achieve wider impact in many ways, including expanding its operations, introducing or developing technologies that spread, developing and using approaches that are then adopted by other NGOs and by government, influencing changes in government and in the policies and actions of donors, and gaining and disseminating understanding about development.

Realising the strengths of NGOs, the federal government identified a number of fields for which they were particularly suited: anti-poverty schemes, land reforms, minimum wages to agricultural workers, bonded labour, the development of scheduled castes and tribes, education, healthcare and family planning, safe drinking water, environment and afforestation, cottage industries, rural housing, women and child development, etc. The role of NGOs seemed to turn overnight from one of charity and welfare to development and empowerment of the poor.

In order to promote voluntary action in village development, the government also decided to set up funding mechanisms (organisations set up and managed by government). The two organisations that first ventured into this field were the Khadi and

Village Industries Commission and the Central Social Welfare Boards. Later, the ministries of rural development, education, health, environment, women and child and science and technology followed suit. In 1986, a unique arms-length organisation of the Ministry of Rural Development was created in the form of the Council for Advancement of People's Action & Rural Technology (CAPART), with the purpose of funding NGOs working in rural development and coordinating NGO activities in the country. Another body, the National Wastelands Development Board, was set up to fund activities in wasteland development through afforestation. The District Rural Development Agencies (DRDAs), which were created at the district level, also fund NGOs working in such areas as watershed development. Both these agencies, at the time of writing the book, have been closed or are temporarily not functioning due to large-scale dishonesty. A senior bureaucrat admitted that it is best to close down such institutions than waste public money.

NGOs in India can be divided into two groups: those that concentrate on the empowerment of people and those engaged in service delivery. The former are involved in training people, making them aware of social issues and government programmes, thereby helping them organise themselves. The most independent of the NGOs avoid being dependent on government for funds and prefer to engage in the less glamorous role of working with the people, empowering them and building their capabilities. Unfortunately, there aren't many of these. A large number of NGOs today are less involved with people and take up the creation of physical assets such as the construction of low-cost housing, building village roads, sinking handpumps, etc., which were traditionally done by the government through contractors and are fund-driven.

Historically, NGOs have acquired funds from diverse sources. For small, local, community-based voluntary organisations, local contributions were the main source. For larger initiatives, funds have come from richer members of society, religious institutions, trusts and business concerns, many of whom contribute with an eye on the tax benefits that such ventures attract. However, these contributions towards funding the NGOs in post-Independence India have been rather limited, the bulk coming from the federal government and foreign funding sources (FFSs).

Over the years, financial support from government has increased steadily. It is estimated that, during the seventh Five Year Plan (1985-90), the federal government spent about ₹500 million each year through NGOs; this has increased to more than ₹2 billion. Targets for expenditure are fixed for each department and failure to achieve them is viewed adversely. Government funding for NGOs is thus not difficult to obtain.

NGOs are sometimes ambivalent about receiving funds from foreign funding agencies. Although ideologically some of them would be shy about approaching foreign funding sources, NGOs can be swayed by simpler and faster clearance of applications in comparison with slothful and often corrupt government agencies. However, many foreign funding sources prefer not to have direct contact in the field and leave the decision of field agency selection and networking to a larger Indian NGO.

Government agencies have evolved a basic set of criteria for funding and evaluation, which can be summed up as follows:

- The NGO should be a society registered under one of the various Acts enacted for the purpose. It should have been in existence and worked at the grassroots level for at least three years and have a bank account and audited statement of accounts certified by a chartered accountant. It should have a good track record of people's participation and worked with them in helping the disadvantaged sections of society.

- Administrative costs should be limited to 10 per cent of the total budget. (Restrictions imposed could include that government will not fund overheads or the running costs of an NGO. Although it provides for programme activities in the field, it could refuse to cover costs such as building or maintenance, staff salaries in full, communication, staff development training, auditing and account-keeping.)

- Funding is available for specific schemes and programmes, largely formulated by the government within its own policies and framework of development. It is rare that a proposal evolved by an NGO on its own can receive funding from a government agency. It is only since June 1998 that CAPART has been permitted to fund innovative projects even if they are not within government guidelines.

- Monitoring and evaluation by government funding agencies is usually done at three stages: pre-funding, mid-term and end of project. The pre-funding stage is the most important in which the organisational profile (also called Transparency Form) of the NGO is looked at. The project is approved only if this is found satisfactory in terms of good track record and capability to mobilise and work with the people's participation for the disadvantaged sections of society. Mid-term evaluation is done after the first installment has been used. The project ends formally only after the utilisation certificate is received from the society and the project has been evaluated by the funding agency.

Accreditation

Given the size of India and the exponential growth of the non-governmental sector (NGOs are estimated to number 1 million, of which 500,000 are active), different funding agencies have evolved their own criteria and mechanism for approaching the most suitable partners. For example, most of the foreign funding sources, through a process of dialogue and adjustment, shortlist one or more states for intervention, depending on their developmental and strategic interests. The identification and selection of partners depends, more often than not, on recommendations from other bilateral aid agencies or from existing NGO partners. Those with no back-up references or from outside the area of operation of a particular donor find it almost impossible to break into the circle.

The federal government ministries, on the other hand, are mandated to have a nationwide spread of projects and they cultivate a thinly spread but well-defined constituency of good performers. The selection is based on past experience, merit and mutual appreciation. For example, the NGO constituency of the Department of Science and Technology (DST) typically operates like a mutual appreciation club. The same, by and large, holds true of several bilateral donors who find it both low-risk and convenient to deal only with known entities. With this in mind, several funding agencies both national and international have compiled their own national directories of Indian NGOs. It is interesting that no more than 10-20 per cent entries overlap.

The Indian NGO sector is vast and as varied as a patchwork quilt. NGOs range the ideological spectrum from extreme right to radical left. There are also many rudderless NGOs that are entirely fund-induced and which mushroomed during the 1980s and 1990s. A sizeable number of these may have no ideology, nor

151

genuine commitment to either welfare or development. Because of this, attempts to rate an NGO can be frustrating, made worse by parallel mushrooming of national and international funding agencies, each with its own agenda and individual yardstick for classifying NGOs as good, bad or indifferent. An organisation which the author founded along with stalwarts of the non-profit sector called the Credibility Alliance was formed and set up norms for good governance and financial accountability. (http://www.credibilityalliance.org). However, few NGOs have taken to it and many will say that even NGOs do not wish to be transparent.

Street action

Direct street action in the form of demonstrations, gherao (protesters occupying the offices) of public officials and street theatre to educate the public is common. Permission must be obtained from the local administration so that they can make arrangements to prevent breach of law and to maintain public order. By and large, all major cities have well-identified areas for such protests and demonstrations. Permission is granted routinely and is easy to get except in cases where the authorities foresee serious breach of law and order and require extra precautions to be taken.

Public Interest Litigation

Traditionally and historically, the rule of law has had significant status in India, and the people and organisations in the country have faith in the judicial system. As regards the nature of the laws, there is legislation to cover virtually every aspect of human existence. There are several vital laws that have traditionally sought to protect individual liberty and freedom. Over the past few years, the higher judiciary in India has acquired an activist dimension, seeking to redress the grievances of the people by nudging, and even coercing, the executive into action. For this, the instrument of Public Interest Litigation (PIL) has empowered the underprivileged in several ways. In essence, even a simple letter in the mail that highlights a grievance or a public wrong can be treated as adequate cause for a PIL, which then gives the judiciary cause to goad the public services into urgent, time-specific action.

Significantly, several of these cases have originated as a result of the participation of NGOs. Because of their commitment, resources and grassroots approach, NGOs are in a unique position to draw the attention of the courts to any kind of irregularity in the implementation of public policies that they encounter. The Chipko Andolan (literally, movement to hug trees), started by Sunderlal Bahuguna with the involvement of women, generated awareness in India and abroad about the fragile ecosystem in the Himalayas. More recently, due to the unstinting efforts of some NGOs, the Supreme Court of India has ordered a ban on all tree-felling in India; this was considered a landmark judgment that has gone a long way towards enforcing accountability among errant Forest Department officials.

The Narmada Bachao Andolan (movement against the construction of a large dam on the river Narmada, which will displace over 250,000 people), spearheaded by Medha Patkar, raised a strong voice against tribal displacement caused by government policies with respect to relief and rehabilitation in the context of the construction of large dams. Another campaign, begun in Rajasthan by Aruna Roy, concerning the rightful payment of wages by the government to its workers employed in the drought programme, led to the Right to Information campaign through the country and has resulted in the enactment of legislation on the subject.

Thus, NGOs have come to occupy a vital position in strengthening the sinews of civil society in India by generating awareness and enforcing public accountability. India has a vibrant NGO sector for a developing country. This is part of the steady institutionalisation of democratic systems in the country and is no less significant than the emergence of democratic decentralisation in rural areas in the form of Panchayati Raj. The proportion of government spending through this sector is minuscule in comparison with its regular expenditure, but is likely to increase substantially because the importance of involving the people in sustainable development is now appreciated. Moreover, it is expected that the significantly higher rate of growth over the past few years, following the adoption of a new economic policy by the federal government, will result in more funds being earmarked for social development.

Another encouraging factor has been the realisation by the NGO sector of the dangers of being over-dependent on funding, especially from foreign sources. Funding cannot be taken for granted or assumed to be available for ever. All NGOs of standing have started to concentrate on fundraising and putting in place sustainable systems, not only for themselves but also for their projects, by their emphasis on withdrawal strategies and handing over management to the local people.

NGOs working on environmental issues

There are many NGOs working on environmental issues. The last directory produced by Developmental Alternatives, founded by the legendary Ashok Khosla, highlighted almost 50,000 NGOs working in the field of environment. India's environmental crisis looms and much of its 346 million hectares (ha) is under varying degrees of stress. The Technology Mission on Wastelands has warned that 175 million ha are virtually unusable and that, unless something drastic is done, India may face greater food shortages.

Land

A crisis often presents the biggest opportunity to bring about change. The greatest success of India's environmental movement, which began with the Chipko Movement of the early 1970s, founded by Chandi Prasad Bhatt and Sunderlal Bahuguna, has been to demonstrate that it can reverse the degradation of land resources. The Dasholi Gram Swarajya Sangh founded by Chandi Prasad Bhatt in Chamoli district showed that land degradation can be reversed. The famines in Maharashtra in the 1970s spurred Vilas Salunke, an engineer and industrialist, to conceive Pani Panchayats people's institutions managing water resources in an equitable manner by ensuring that the community's grouping patterns matched the availability of water resources. This was water management in which equity and sustainability were combined. Ralegan Siddhi of Anna Hazare also showed that villages can become self-sustaining and environmental destruction can be reversed.

In the mid-1970s, Krishna Bhaurao Hazare (Anna Hazare) retired to his destitute village, Ralegan Siddhi, and began to mobilise the community to manage its village natural resource base on principles similar to those of Pani Panchayats. Around the same time, in Sukhomajri, a village near Chandigarh, PR Mishra, a government scientist, was trying to convince the villagers to accept his technocratic soil conservation efforts. In the late 1970s, he began a participatory approach that was close to that of Pani Panchayats and Ralegan Siddhi. He was one of the icons of the Indian Against Corruption movement of 2012.

By the mid-1980s, the federal government had begun to wake up to the crisis of environmental degradation and rural poverty. In 1985, Prime Minister Rajiv Gandhi announced the establishment of the National Wastelands Development Board and gave it the daunting target of afforesting 5 million ha a year through people's movement helped by government agencies. In 1989, *Towards Green Villages*, published by the Centre for Science and Environment, spelled out a general strategy to replicate the local successes of Sukhomajri and Ralegan Siddhi. In 1992, Prime Minister Narasimha Rao announced the establishment of a Department of Wastelands Development. It was decided that money being spent on rural employment programmes should go to watershed development, but state governments were slow to respond. The problem was how to mould a rigid and compartmentalised bureaucracy to promote a highly participatory strategy for water and forest management. Many watershed programmes launched in the 1980s had failed.

A breakthrough finally came in the mid-1980s in Madhya Pradesh. Inspired by the achievements in Ralegan Siddhi, Chief Minister Digvijaya Singh pushed his bureaucracy to find ways to promote a people's movement for watershed development by using money provided by using money provided by the Centre for rural employment schemes. By the late 1990s, Singh had reached out to 8,000 villages—representing nearly 1 per cent of India's land area. Of all the districts, nowhere has the regeneration been more stunning than in Jhabua, whose land had looked like that of the moon. In 1998, this effort had even brought Singh a pleasant and surprising political reward: his party was returned to power despite all predictions to the contrary.

This is dramatic transformation although these high points of rural regeneration challenges are far from being the norm. It took 200 years of misgovernance and, consequently, a steady decline to reach to the conditions of the 1970s. However, it has taken India only 20 years to learn how to bring about change. Hopefully, if the country's political system also realises that India's villagers provide political blessings to those who try to deal with their ecological poverty, electoral democracy will ensure that future change will spread even faster.

The challenge before society is to ensure that the village republic paradigm becomes the norm nationwide. There is no reason why India cannot regenerate all its degraded lands and get rid of the abject poverty that currently remains as a blot on the country.

Indian villages are highly integrated ecological systems. What happens in one component invariably has an impact on the others. However, this finely tuned system can easily fall apart. If too many trees are cut or the pressures of a growing population reduce the area of forests and grazing lands, there will be a shortage of firewood. This will force people to burn cow dung as cooking fuel, leaving little manure to fertilize crop lands. Moreover, as the source of fodder declines, animals will starve and so will not produce cow dung. The area will soon look like a desert.

India already has 129.78 million ha of wasteland, of which 35.92 million ha are degraded forest land and 93.86 million ha are degraded non-forest land. What the country desperately needs is an approach that increases in a sustainable manner the productivity of all the components of the village ecosystem.

The only way to end the fragmented approaches to rural

development is to promote integrated village ecosystem planning and management. This can be attempted only at the village level, village by village, because there is enormous diversity in Indian village ecosystems. Even in one overall ecosystem, the agro-system of a village can vary greatly. Besides, the task of planning for an individual village can be achieved rapidly and judiciously. Mahatma Gandhi said that a village should be the primary unit of planning in India and that villagers should be educated in a manner that would equip them with the capacity to better their own health as well as that of the village, and to improve their productivity and economy.

However, this vision of self-sufficient villages, which would transform the land and the social life of millions of Indian villagers, has yet to become reality. With increasing degradation of land, large sections of the rural populace have been migrating to cities in search of work. The vast majority of our rural population remains below the poverty line. Various development programmes have failed because they have been implemented without people's participation. Nevertheless, there is a ray of hope in this gloomy scenario: there are now numerous instances of village regeneration through people's participation.

One example of community land management working wonders is that of Sukhomajri village in Haryana, located in the foothills of the Shivalik. This village was bone dry two decades ago. Then, spurred by soil scientist PR Mishra, the people of Sukhomajri took it upon themselves to rejuvenate the land. They achieved this through what Mishra calls the cyclical mode of development—i.e. cyclical growth results if villagers reinvest their savings from regenerated land for further ecological improvements. Sukhomajri has become an inspiration for villagers all over India, and is regarded the world over as a model village for sustainable development. It is the greatest success story in community forest management. When all eyes in rural India gaze skywards for the monsoon, farmers in Sukhomajri remain unperturbed, knowing they are no longer at the mercy of the rain god. The village has freed itself from poverty and malnutrition that are so common in most of rural India. Sukhomajri, once a dry village, became green, prosperous and self-reliant.

The model of development used by Sukhomajri has been replicated in other villages of Haryana, Punjab and Bihar. The village has evoked considerable interest among policymakers, NGOs, international funding agencies and researchers. For some, it has become a temple of modern India; for others a learning ground. However, with growing prosperity and fame, numerous problems have also crept into the village. Unfortunately, things are deteriorating because of the reemergence of the bureaucratic mindset that believes that illiterate villagers cannot care for their resources.

The principle behind the transformation of Sukhomajri was to enhance agricultural production to meet the daily needs of villagers, such as fuel wood, fodder and food grain; surplus would be sold. However, the emphasis currently is on maximising production of bhaber (an increasingly valuable wild grass traditionally used for rope-making, but also in great demand from paper mills). This is done at the expense of the villagers' needs, because they are not allowed to cut mungeri (young bhaber) to feed their livestock during the lean months of July to September.

The Sukhomajri experiment can be termed a success because it proved that—with community planning, commitment and restraint—the economy of a village can be turned around. Tree density in the village increased from 13 per hectare in 1976 to 1,272 per hectare in 1992. Grass increased from 40 kilogramme per hectare (kg/ha) in 1972 to 3,000 kg/ha in 1992. The village sold the extra grass.

As the grass and trees regenerated in the watershed, the villagers began to get more fodder. They sold goat and bought high-yielding buffalo. While the number of goat decreased from 246 to 10 between 1975 and 1986, the number of buffaloes increased from 79 to 291. The milk yield in the village rose from 2.23 litres per animal a day in 1977 to 3.01 litres in 1986. The milk production of the village increased from 334 litres per day in 1977 to 579 litres in 1986. The villagers began to sell milk worth ₹350,000 a year. In 1989, the village became the first in India to be levied income tax on its earnings from regenerated forest. The average annual household income also increased from ₹10,000 in 1979 to ₹15,000 in 1984.

Sukhomajri taught environmentalists that in many cases the starting point for environmental regeneration should be water and not trees. Once a small water-harvesting system has been built and an equitable system has been developed to share the water, the village community will immediately see the benefits of protecting its water system by controlled grazing and by planting trees and grass. Slowly, one thing will lead to another, and the community will start managing its entire ecosystem.

Community land management has also transformed Jhabua, a poor tribal district of Madhya Pradesh, from a moonscape a few years ago to a sea of green. This is an outstanding example, as it is an effort by a state government to involve the people in managing their land and water resources, with excellent results. Unlike

Sukhomajri, where bureaucratic interference soon started having negative effects, in Jhabua the people are involved in the concept, planning, implementation and maintenance of land and watershed activities. There is good coordination among the district officials and the villagers.

The Madhya Pradesh government launched the Rajiv Gandhi Mission for Watershed Development (RGMWD) in Jhabua in October 1994. It came with a healing touch, mending the scars of a ravaged area. A decentralised mission with a deadline, it started with the objective of improving 1.2 million ha by 2000 over several watersheds, each watershed project finishing within four years. The mission broke all rules. The people, instead of bureaucrats, became the decision-makers. They envisaged greening more than 2.9 million ha approximately 1 per cent of the country's total land area spanning 6,691 villages, through 5,024 watersheds.

The RGMWD that was introduced in 42 of the state's 45 districts has transformed the local economy. In three years, some 14 million days of employment have been created all over the state. Soon, 218 small watersheds covered 124,000 ha in Jhabua, at an estimated cost of ₹444.7 billion, funded through 12 governmental and seven non-governmental project implementing agencies (PIAs). (The RGMWD is funded by both the state and central governments.)

Jhabua has become the model district for watershed management. The land in Jhabua is being greened and the lost forests are undergoing natural regeneration. The ecological change has also improved the economy. In 1997, the district—which had a migration rate of 60 per cent and an acute shortage of fodder recorded its lowest ever migration of 30 per cent. It also sold surplus fodder worth tens of thousands of rupees in nearby districts, including Gujarat, from where Jhabua used to buy fodder.

Water

For thousands of years, India has had a tradition of worshipping rivers. However, even the river—worshipping Hindus do not think twice before polluting a river. The Bharatiya Janata Party (BJP), a political party that claims to draw inspiration from Hinduism, did not regard the mucking up of the Ganga and Yamuna or of the numerous temple tanks as an issue for a long time. This despite the fact that the BJP-led coalition had announced water to be a key issue on its national agenda.

India has turned its back on its rivers. The assault on the rivers from population growth, agricultural modernisation, urbanisation and industrialisation is enormous and growing daily. The increasing pollution of India's rivers thus constitutes the biggest threat to public health. Since Independence, neglect of water resources has killed more than 50 million children, and now even adults will begin to die of horrendous diseases because of the growing chemical pollution. Although the Central Water Commission (CWC) says that development of water resources has been given 'pride of place in all five-year plans', water resources bear the brunt of unplanned urbanisation and rapid industrialisation. Rajendra Singh, Magsaysay Award winner and known as India's 'waterman', is leading a Ganga Mukti Abhiyan to clean the Ganga of encroachments and pollution by various authorities. Rajendra Singh began his work with an NGO called Tarun Bharat Sangh in Alwar district of Rajasthan where he restored old dry rivers through embankments, water recharge and plantations. In the early 1980s, river pollution in India had reached a crisis. Unfortunately, the situation has only worsened. Urban planning remains low on the nation's list of priorities, and sewage and wash waters from most human settlements enter the nearest body of water often without treatment. For instance, in 1982 it was reported by the Centre for Science and Environment (CSE) in its *First Citizen's Report on the State of India's Environment* that large quantities of sewage from Delhi's drains were being discharged into the Yamuna without proper treatment, rendering the river unfit for use between Delhi and Agra. Since then, attempts to cleanse the river have been nullified by the extremely polluted waters released into it by Delhi's drains, prompting the Chairperson of the Central Pollution Control Board (CPCB) to remark that even if the government were to spend many millions on cleaning up the river, the Yamuna would still remain polluted. Barring the efforts of the CSE and Rajendra Singh, there seems to be no plan to clean up our rivers. If ever rivers change, it will be due to civil society's efforts.

Rajendra Singh began his efforts with the Tarun Bharat Sangh in Gopalpura village near Thanagazi in Alwar teaching children and school dropouts. Singh found children were always busy getting water for their homes and could not concentrate on school. A village elder Mangubaba shared a pearl of wisdom saying that "if water is provided all other things will inevitably follow; other things are available in the market but not water." This touched a chord in Singh's heart and the objectives became clearer to him. Under the guidance of Mangubaba he discussed the flow of runoff water and a location was finally decided upon. Singh followed Mangubaba's advice and then got the first Johad a small earthen embankment constructed. Soon the rains came and there was lot of water. He then focused on rain water harvesting structures, changing the landscape of the area. Later many more structures like the Beruji Bandh, the Sankara Bandh and the Lalpura Johad were constructed. Singh later felt that rivers and other sources being polluted needed more attention.

What causes pollution?

Polluting rivers is dangerous because they are the primary source of drinking water for towns and cities downstream of the point of pollution. Broadly, causes of water pollution may be ascribed to:

- urbanisation;
- industrialisation;
- withdrawal of water;
- agricultural runoff and improper agricultural practices;
- religious and social practices.

Many towns and cities that have grown on the banks of a river did not give a thought to the problem of urban sewage. Most of it is conveniently allowed to flow into the rivers. The 25 large towns and cities on the Ganga, for instance, generate 1.34 billion litres of sewage a day. Before the Ganga Action Plan (GAP), over 95 per cent of this entered the river without being treated. In addition, there has been a rapid increase in industrial pollution at these urban centres. Effluent from industries, often containing toxins and heavy metals, drains into the rivers, which become the source of drinking water for towns downstream.

Municipal water treatment facilities in India do not at present remove traces of heavy metals. Given the fact that heavily polluted rivers are the major source of municipal water for most towns and cities along their course, it is believed that over the years, every consumer has been exposed to unknown quantities of pollutants in the water they have consumed.

Industrial waste or effluent pollutes most Indian rivers and streams. All this industrial waste is toxic to life forms that consume the water.

Withdrawal of water for irrigation and other purposes leaves almost no water in the rivers. The only water left in them is that from sewers, drains and seepage of ground water. The Yamuna, for example, has almost no water at Tajewala in Haryana, where the Eastern Yamuna Canal and the Western Yamuna Canal abstract all the water for irrigation. Similarly, the upper and the lower Ganga Canals have left the Ganga downstream dry.

Agricultural run-off and improper agricultural practices result in traces of fertilizers and pesticides being washed into the nearest body of water during the monsoons or when there are heavy showers. Because such agricultural inputs are diffused through the river basin, they are called non-point sources of pollution.

After rivers recede at the end of monsoon, the riverbeds are coated with fresh deposits of silt and provide an ideal farming area. Yet, this ancient practice has now become dangerous because the fertilizers and pesticides used on these tracts of land are bound to be washed into rivers during the monsoons. In 1997, the Supreme Court ordered the government of Uttar Pradesh to prevent riverbed farming upstream of the Yamuna water intake point in Agra, and to stop cattle owners from watering their animals in the rivers.

Religious and social practices contribute to pollution. For example, the carcasses of cattle and other animals are disposed of in the so-called holy rivers. In keeping with ancient rituals, the dead are still cremated on riverbanks. Mass bathing in rivers during religious festivals is another environmentally harmful practice. Studies have indicated that the biochemical oxygen demand (BOD) rises when tens of thousands of people simultaneously take a holy dip. Religious practices also demand that offerings from a puja be immersed in a river. It is now common to see people immersing offerings in plastic bags, further adding to the pollution of a river.

The federal government has done little to prevent the

situation from becoming worse. The CPCB has well-constructed, scientifically competent studies on almost all Indian rivers. However, when it comes to action, the government has been woefully inept. Tackling river pollution was a non-issue until the GAP was launched.

Launched in 1985, the GAP was the largest ever clean-up operation in India. But it proved be a sorry tale. The plan was criticised for misuse of funds, overspending and slow progress: the Ganga apparently was as dirty as ever, with little improvement in water quality. In 1991 came GAP Phase II, to complete the work left over from the first phase of the Plan. This programme aimed at cleaning not only the mighty Ganga but also its tributaries Yamuna, Gomti and Damodar. Thus the Yamuna Action Plan, Gomti Action Plan and Damodar Action Plan were added. In 1995 the government launched the National River Conservation Plan (NRCP), which has all river clean-up plans in its ambit.

The biggest drawback of river-cleaning programmes such as GAP is the failure to think of where the money for treatment facilities in the long run would come from. With power supply to most Indian towns being erratic, the facilities, which are heavily dependent on power, are underused, undoing all attempts to clean the rivers. NRCP, set up with GAP as its role model, failed to rectify these shortcomings. Moreover, river-cleaning programmes do not address the problem of pollution resulting from agricultural run-off. Unfortunately, despite all its efforts, the federal government has had little success in preventing the situation from getting worse. Both GAP and the NRCP lack participation by the people and a political will, especially of cash-strapped state governments.

Nevertheless, there has been a change in water quality of the rivers since river-cleaning schemes have been launched. Although mostly unnoticed by the average person, researchers confirm there has been improvement in water quality.

Dams

By the mid-1980s, following protests against huge dams, it was clear that mega dams were generating immense social and ecological problems from forced displacement of people to ecological destruction of catchment areas. The government has since rejected many dam proposals, and has even scrapped several more after public protests, especially in cases where the ecological impact would have been high. But where the protests have largely centered on forced displacement, the government has stuck to its guns. The projects continue to limp ahead despite repeated protests. A humane rehabilitation policy that would be acceptable to all parties concerned remains elusive.

Although the anti-dam movement reached a crescendo with an international campaign that forced the federal government to opt out of World Bank support for the Sardar Sarovar dam, India's water managers have not yet revised their strategies for water supply and hydro power. As a result, the protests have slowed progress on dam construction and investment. Resistance to change has been equally strong, and even sensitive politicians have not been able come up with good ideas on how to develop a new and sustainable water resource programme.

An interesting development has been the emergence of struggles of people affected by dams built years ago. It is now acknowledged that none of the people ousted by the dams built in the past few decades whether the Pong dam in Himachal Pradesh or Panshet in Maharashtra have been properly resettled. Now, encouraged by the success of dam struggles, the people displaced by dams are organising themselves, demanding that they be resettled preferably on the banks of the rivers. Examples include the Bargi Bandh Visthapit Avam Prabhavit Sangh (Bargi dam completed in 1990 on the Narmada river) and the Mahi-Kadana dam (Gujarat, Rajasthan, completed in 1978, on the Mahi river).

Damming the Narmada has been one of the most cited examples in the debate on development versus people. Its river basin has been the subject of both pro- and anti-dam activists at various national and international fora. Amid the debate over the height of dams, their economic viability and the rehabilitation of people displaced, a highlight has been the people's organised struggle against non-participatory planning. It has also brought centre stage the issue of a national rehabilitation and resettlement policy. The Narmada Bachao Andolan was led by Medha Patkar who brought this centrestage and even forced the World Bank to retract from the project after the famous Morse report which damned the feasibility exercise of the government as full of exaggeration and inflated benefits. Similar doubts have been expressed over the Tehri Dam and other dams across the country. It forced the government to relook its EIA (environmental impact assessment) process and the public hearing of displaced people. The Tehri dam experience in Uttarakhand has highlighted the urgent need for scientific and socio-economic assessment of mega projects in the country. Tehri is witness to noted environmentalist Sunderlal Bahuguna's continuing crusade against the dam. But his single-handed attempt to stall its construction yielded no significant result. The dam submerged the small town of Tehri. The cost of ₹19.2 billion (₹192 crore) projected in 1978 had reached ₹60 billion (₹6,000 crore) in 1998.

It is obvious that it will be even more difficult to build dams. Population growth alone will ensure that. A catchment that had

10,000 people at the time of Independence now has more than 30,000. The greater the number of people displaced, the bigger the problem of their relocation, and lesser the land available elsewhere for them to go. Many project sites may be devoid of people, but then they are likely to have rich forests as in central India, the Western Ghats or the eastern Himalayan ranges. The seismic instability of the Himalayan range, which otherwise has numerous possible dam sites, poses another set of problems.

Nonetheless, a growing India needs water for its people, its farms and its factories. Food security depends on water as much as ecological security depends on good water use. Hydroelectric projects are a good way to produce non-polluting energy, which India needs. Balancing the increasing demands on limited water resources through population and economic growth with ecological and social security is therefore a challenging task. It would not be wrong to say that India's environmental movement in general, and its anti-dam component in particular, having successfully lodged its protest against a range of dam projects, now faces an even tougher task in the years ahead: how can it help India visualise and develop a strategy for sustainable water development and use?

Forests

In the 1980s and 1990s India was quite successful in reducing the rate of deforestation and stabilising forest cover. Forest depletion in India has since been arrested to some extent. Nevertheless, natural forest declined from 55.12 million ha in 1980 to 51.73 million ha in 1990, according to the Food and Agriculture Organisation. Moreover, forests still face major challenges and threats from natural pests, timber smugglers and poor management.

Environmentalists and forest managers are keen on protecting the nation's forests. But they are not clear on what they want to protect. This aspect is relevant because forest monitoring data must reflect the needs and objectives of a programme. The 'India State of the Forest' reports published by the Ministry of Environment and Forests give regular updates in terms of changes in the total forest, dense forest and open forest.

Dense forests cover only 12 per cent of India's land area, which is much less than the target of 33 per cent. Moreover, not much is known about the composition of dense forests. If a large part consists of plantation, the appropriate policy for it would be to develop and log dense forests to serve economic needs. The part that consists of regenerated natural growth requires a separate set of management objectives. Undisturbed pristine forest cover probably contains immense biodiversity and must be zealously protected against human exploitation. Unfortunately, there is precious little information on where such forests still exist and what the current pressures are on them. In a country of over 300 million ha, pristine forests probably cover less than 10 million ha.

Once this ecologically invaluable part of the forest estate has been located and documented, an even bigger challenge will be to devise a management plan to protect it. Given that India has a high and growing population density and an economy with a voracious appetite for forest resources, no management plan will succeed unless it involves the people and provides them with adequate incentives. But what incentives can mere protection provide? The answer is obviously difficult, but it can be found.

The looting and smuggling of sandalwood forests in the south has revealed a deep-rooted problem with India's forest management. People living in the forests have no interest in protecting forests. Little is known about the scale of timber smuggling and its impact on forest resources. Getting people and forests together is, thus, the biggest challenge facing the country's forest estate today. Although the government has made considerable strides in involving people in regenerating degraded forest lands, it has yet to develop a strategy to involve people in protecting what already exists.

Private plantation companies could have met the demand for teak by growing trees outside forest land. But they lost credibility because they became greedy. Investors may lose as much as ₹25 billion (₹2,500 crore). Inadequate responses to several outbreaks of forest diseases indicate that the government is not investing adequately in forest sciences. The forestry bureaucracy's answer to the sal borer crisis was large-scale felling of infested trees in November 1997.

Atmosphere

History has an amazing way of repeating itself but most people tend to learn little from it. By the mid-1950s, just about a decade into the economic boom after World War II, most cities of Europe, Japan and the US were reeling under air pollution and gasping for breath. It was only in the 1970s that the situation began to improve in a few cities after the respective governments initiated action.

The genesis of the problem of air pollution in the developed countries in the 1950s can be traced to the Western economic model, which is built on intensive use of fossil fuel energy and materials and is, therefore, a toxic model. The toxicity can be controlled only through high investment in pollution control as well as political and social discipline. However, the same toxicity is now affecting the developing world, especially those countries, including India, that are witnessing Western-style economic growth.

India has seen a phenomenal increase in the number of industries and vehicles in the past decade, along with the mushrooming of cities. As a consequence, there has been a dramatic deterioration in the quality of urban air in most regions of the country. There has been a proliferation of regional hotspots with severe pollution in the past decade. Even in small towns, air pollution has been unpredictably high.

The unprecedented growth in the number of vehicles in India has emerged as the most significant contributor to the poisoning of urban air. Industrial air pollution is localised in nature, bringing entire cities into the grip of severe air pollution.

The rise in common pollutants is alarming. Short-term monitoring by various research organisations has confirmed that they have reached dangerous levels in the air of a range of towns. The common pollutants in urban air include sulphur dioxide (SO_2), nitrogen oxide (NO_2) and suspended particulate matter (SPM). There is serious threat also from a range of other pollutants such as carbon monoxide (CO), emissions of small particulates, lead, benzene, polycyclic aromatic hydrocarbons (PAH) and ozone.

It is unfortunate that most of the air quality standards in India are well above the guidelines of the World Health Organisation (WHO). Because these standards have been set for individual pollutants, they do not show the combined effect. The WHO, which rates only the megacities of the world, has rated New Delhi the fourth most polluted city in the world. However, compared with other cities of India, New Delhi is not the worst.

India is dotted with pollution hotspots. The surprising topper is Gajroli La a barely known small town in Uttar Pradesh. The problem of air pollution has assumed serious proportions in metros. New Delhi, Kolkata and Chennai have already been rated fourth, sixth and thirteenth among the 41 most polluted megacities in SPM concentration. Vehicular emissions are largely responsible for high levels of SPM.

The poor air quality of urban India indicates total lack of planning. Legislation to deal with the problem has come only as kneejerk reaction to serious episodes of accidental industrial gas leaks such as the Bhopal disaster. But a steady and alarming dip in air quality over the years in almost all the towns and cities of India continues unnoticed. As a result, planning lacks coherent vision to deal with all sources of pollution.

What little legal development took place up to the 1990s was myopically focused on stationary sources of pollution such as industries and thermal power plants. It remained almost blind to the looming air pollution crisis from moving sources such as vehicles regulations to deal with vehicular emissions came into force only in 1990.

Until recently, fuel quality was barely held responsible for vehicular pollution in Indian cities. Fuel standards with respect to factors that have a bearing on the emission levels became fully operational late in 2000. The Supreme Court of India passed a judgment that vehicles should be converted to run on compressed natural gas or CNG, which is less polluting, and that vehicles older than 15 years should not be used in Delhi.

Despite the spate of legal reforms, the goal of good quality air has remained elusive; air quality has steadily worsened. As planning remains fundamentally flawed, a few fragmented laws cannot help to clean the air. There is a need for focused planning and disciplined enforcement.

The role of the federal government is largely confined to setting up air quality and emission standards for vehicles and industries, and for fuel quality. The government has attempted to control air pollution in Delhi. To prevent the nightmare of smog and the resulting need for gasmasks, the numbers of vehicles will have to be controlled. This is something all state governments have failed to do.

The government has approached the problem of industrial pollution at two levels by setting emission standards for industries and by land use plans to segregate industries from residential areas. But on both counts, enforcement has encountered serious problems. The effort of government agencies prompted in most cases by legal action has been to order the closure of polluting companies. But, after many such orders, the effectiveness of this strategy is still unknown.

Habitat

Almost every small and medium-sized town in India is on its way to becoming an urban nightmare. From the industrially prosperous Ludhiana in the Punjab to the tourist-rich Jaisalmer in Rajasthan, these towns are beset by the same set of problems. Too much traffic, mushrooming slums, piles of garbage and high levels of air and water pollution are making life hell for residents, and are leading to increasing incidence of health problems. The people most affected are the poor, who are often jobless and have to scrounge around for food and shelter.

Lack of investment in urban infrastructure in these small towns is pushing their residents into the cities, which are already groaning under the pressure of a large population. The situation can only get worse in the face of an apathetic citizenry's acceptance of governmental indifference and the industrial sector's irresponsibility.

India's industrial towns are today being crushed by their own growth. Whether it is Ludhiana, Tiruppur or Jetpur, the environment is paying a heavy price. Unplanned and thoughtless industrialisation has become the bane of all these towns. Industrial units have mushroomed.

Towns have flooded the rivers and ground waters are polluted beyond belief—little aquatic life exists in the Sutlej, Noyyal or Bhaddar rivers. The water in the wells of Choki village in Jetpur looks like paint and the air is redolent of highly noxious fumes. The inhabitants suffer from infectious illnesses such as tuberculosis and skin diseases. According to doctors in Jetpur, the incidence of leukaemia has risen steeply. Almost every third person in Ludhiana complains of bronchitis.

With a large influx of people from long distances, slums have cropped up all over these towns. In Ludhiana, most labour is migrant; the workers travelling from as far as Bihar and Uttar Pradesh. The increasing numbers put pressure not just on the civic facilities but also on overexploited natural resources.

The number of cities with a population of more than 1 million increased from 12 in 1981 to 23 in 1991. Of the people who live in smaller towns and cities, 68 per cent face environmental problems. People in non-industrial towns face habitat problems equalling those in industrial towns. As these cities have grown without corresponding growth in size or civic infrastructure, basic amenities have come under tremendous pressure. Slums are ever-present, with almost non-existent sanitation, healthcare, water or electricity supply. Natural resources are fast disappearing the biggest casualty is, of course water. Ground water levels are dipping alarmingly.

Plastic bags have become a colossal environmental hazard. These virtually indestructible items can be found everywhere in drains, garbage dumps, gardens, on trees and sometimes even in nests. Environmentalists such as Iqbal Malik of Vatavaran say the plastic bag is slowly killing our cities and will soon be doing the same to our rural areas. The national Plastic Management Task Force, set up by the federal government in 1996, recommended a ban on the use of recycled plastic bags. The states of Himachal Pradesh, Haryana, Sikkim and Tamil Nadu have also bannedthe indiscriminate disposal of plastic bags.

Health

Economic development is the watchword for India's march into the twenty-first century. But the nation is paying an enormous price; development has brought in its wake ecological devastation and health problems. A World Bank study estimated that environmental damage amounted to $9.7 billion (about ₹340 billion or ₹34,000 crore) per year or 4.5 per cent of the gross domestic product in 1992. Environmental costs are measured in terms of health costs incurred because of growing air and water pollution, and of lost production because of the degrading of natural resources such as crop lands and grazing lands, as well as deforestation.

Poor water accounts for health costs worth $7 billion a year (₹199.5 billion or ₹19,950 crore), or about 59 per cent of the total environmental costs. Almost all surface water in India (except the mountainous regions) is unfit for human consumption.

India faces a grim future because of air pollution. Although no comprehensive epidemiological study has been conducted to determine how air pollution is affecting health, it is clearly causing respiratory, cardiac and nervous system disorders. Here are some details:

- One out of every 10 schoolchildren in Delhi suffers from asthma;

- Blood lead levels in children living in metros are alarmingly high;
- India spends about ₹46.6 billion (₹4,660 crore) a year to make up for ill-health caused by pollution of ambient air.

However, the pollution with the greatest health consequences remains unseen or overlooked: it affects the silent majority women and children. While benefits of agricultural tools and machinery have spread to most rural populations, changes that improve the working conditions of women in the home remain limited to affluent rural households. Women exposed to wood smoke while cooking inhale huge quantities of harmful pollutants and suffer from alarming health problems. In one of the first studies on domestic pollution conducted in four villages of Gujarat in 1981, average levels of total suspended particulates in indoor air were estimated to be 700 micrograms per cubic metre ($\mu g /m^3$), about ten times higher than the WHO standard of 60-90 $\mu g /m^3$.

Several studies found that women suffer from heart diseases such as corpulmonale (enlargement of the heart) and chronic bronchitis when exposed to wood smoke. The magnitude of domestic pollution was known by the early 1980s, and was documented in CSE's *Second Citizens' Report on the Environment* in 1984-85. The report also indicated that several steps could be taken to reduce exposure to smoke while cooking and thus reduce its adverse impact on health. These steps included increasing the use of alternative biomass fuels such as biogas and charcoal, altering the design of stoves so that exposure to smoke is reduced, and increasing ventilation in the homes of the poor.

Today, the smoke still remains and the walls of the home continue to be covered with soot. The plight of women has not improved an iota. All efforts have focused on epidemiological studies to look further into the links between biomass smoke and health. But little has been achieved in terms of setting and implementing national policies relating to domestic energy and health.

Energy

India lives largely in its rural areas, but the federal government devotes little money to understand and monitor rural India. Rural energy is an area that has been consistently plagued by presumptions. For a long time, foresters have argued that people were meeting their need for firewood by plundering the forests— almost like locusts stripping the crops. In the 1980s, however, rural energy experts pointed out that firewood comes mostly in the form of twigs and branches. How could using these be laying forests bare? Other studies subsequently showed that a lot of firewood was coming from trees in farmland. Therefore, the ransacking of forests had been grossly over-estimated. A survey of the early 1990s has shown that people are using better quality fuel wood than in the late 1970s, and getting more of it from lands than from forests. That is indeed heartening.

But the reasons for this change in different parts of the country are not known; neither is it known whether such changes are permanent or a flash in the pan. There is a clear need to understand better the people in rural India, and on a consistent basis. Otherwise, there is a danger that policy can easily fall behind practice.

Living resources

With problems mounting over national parks and sanctuaries, India's wildlife and protected areas are in jeopardy. The malady in most cases has been identified as the largely unscientific and anti-people approaches of dealing with the management of these regions. India needs a rational, sustainable and effective conservation policy that also cares for people's needs and rights.

India has 521 national parks and sanctuaries that cover 4.3 per cent of its geographical area but policies to conserve wildlife are mostly unscientific. Reserve sitting and management are often based on imported conservation models, which are inappropriate for developing countries, because they have little insight into past and present land use patterns.

Traditional communities have always been dependent on natural resources, including forests. It is therefore natural that they should have rights over the land they have lived in, besides the resources they have used and replenished for centuries. But the Wildlife (Protection) Act 1972, amended in 1991, prohibits human intervention or settlement in national parks, and allows only limited intervention in sanctuaries. Although the government has taxed the local people to pay for biodiversity conservation, it has not guaranteed them benefits from this exercise.

This alienation has triggered a backlash from local communities. In some places, resettlement has manifested itself in the violation of protected areas laws by local inhabitants. It is alleged that, while the laws are enforced against the poor, commercial interests have continuously violated laws often with the connivance of the Forest Department—in plundering forest wealth. In School Paneshwar Sanctuary in Gujarat, for example, people are prevented from taking small amounts of bamboo, while truckloads of bamboo regularly rumble out of the sanctuary, under the benevolent gaze of the authorities, to feed a paper mill nearby. Another example is the proposed Rajaji National Park in Uttar Pradesh. The authorities are desperately trying to evict the few thousand Gujjars living inside the park, while ignoring blatant encroachment and violation of laws by large government-owned industrial complexes and an army ammunition dump. There is therefore growing cynicism about the sincerity of state-managed conservation strategy.

Wildlife management means not just conserving lions and tigers but, more importantly, harmonising the objectives of biodiversity with the rights of the people dependent on these resources. Local policy formulated at national level is bound to run into serious problems with implementation, the ultimate cost being paid by the nation's wildlife and biodiversity. Conservation strategies that assign charges to the people and a specific role to the state and environmentalists would work better than state-managed strategies. It is imperative that the local people become the biggest economic beneficiaries from parks and sanctuaries.

Agents of change

The founding fathers of the Indian nation gave the judiciary the right to stop any law or executive action that went against the spirit of the Constitution. But India's judges might not have foreseen that a time would come when they would be forcing the executive to take existing laws seriously.

With environmental problems growing by leaps and bounds and environmental governance institutions failing to meet the challenge, India's biggest strength its democracy was beginning to assert itself by the mid-1970s. By the mid-1980s, even Prime Minister Rajiv Gandhi had realised that public intervention was necessary to resolve the conflict between environment and development. He pointed out several times in 1986 that he had intervened to ensure that people were given the right to take polluters to court under the Environment Protection Act, a law that was enacted during his tenure.

Around the same time, India's judges were also starting to address the growing crisis. Justice PN Bhagwati interpreted that the right to life guaranteed in the Constitution included the right to healthy environment. Other judgments allowed public-spirited citizens to petition the judges against environmental damage. All of this soon gave rise to a powerful movement in litigation. This development gave many a ray of hope in an otherwise growing environment of cynicism and despair. Judges have closed polluting companies and environmentally harmful prawn (aqua) farms, mandated cleaner fuel for vehicles, and protected forests and architectural treasures such as the Taj Mahal. Not only the Supreme Court but also the High Courts have actively supported public interest petitions.

Unfortunately, every new effort has its own problems. Court orders have often proved ineffective because of the poor advice that the judiciary has received from government agencies and the lawyers who filed the petitions. The inability of government agencies to deliver effective action added to it. But the orders which aim to set up special authorities to monitor government commitments and regularly advise the courts on action that needs to be taken are a step forward in improving environmental governance. India can only hope that, where lawmakers and bureaucrats have failed, judges will be able to solve the problems.

Corruption

Why are there so many schools without teachers? Hospitals without good medical facilities? Roads built so badly? Why is so little attention paid to measures that ensure the efficient use of water in government irrigation projects? Why is decentralisation and transparency in government decision-making opposed so strongly? Why are government rules and procedures so convoluted and cumbersome?

There could be a million answers to these questions. But corruption is common to all of them. It permeates the entire establishment and society, and affects everyone's lives. The environment the nation's natural estate does not escape the effect of corruption.

When corruption is rampant, the government will focus on construction and procurement because this is where the big money is but not on high-quality construction or on good use of the facilities created. The focus is on the hardware and not on the software. When corruption is rampant, protecting anything air, rivers, forests, wildlife becomes difficult. When laws are cumbersome, as in the case of felling a nationalised tree, everyone needs a fixer to smooth the procedures. Corruption affects not only the environment but also the poor. Few know that the blinding of criminals by the Bhagalpur police in the 1980s was the result of corruption in land allocation in the peculiar environment of moving riverine islands. One thing led to another. Corruption led to marginalisation of the poor, which led to alienation and violent reprisals, which in turn led to police repression. As long as there is corruption, it will be difficult to protect the natural estate, prevent pollution or manage the environment.

Decentralisation and corruption also have a peculiar relationship. The corrupt love decentralisation but only up to their level. Nobody who is corrupt wants decentralisation to levels below them. The structure of regulation has led to patronage at every level, leading to levels of corruption. Much of the destruction of the environment can be traced to this mindless regulation that leads to the distortion of governance.

Developing governance systems that reduce corruption is perhaps the biggest challenge for India in the twenty-first century. A simple answer lies in reducing the role of the state as a provider in our daily lives and involving the citizens in regulating the use of the environment. Participatory management and participatory regulation. But all this will happen only after a long struggle. The moderation of greed and the application of just needs are more appropriate today than ever before. Many NGOs moved into the space provided by the Right to Information (RTI) and its implementation, commonly referred to as RTI activists. Civil society tried to empower the masses for political actionthrough participatory methods. The methods were innovative and unfamiliar to the current political class. While transparency in government became inevitable, many NGOs did not want to be transparent.

CHAPTER 5

NEED FOR ACCOUNTABILITY
IN CIVIL SOCIETY SECTOR

*We are conscious of only an insignificant portion
of our being; for the most part we are unconscious.
It is this unconsciousness that keeps us down to our
un-regenerate nature and prevents changes and
transformation in it. It is through unconsciousness
that the un-divine (and un-virtuous) forces enter into
us and make us their slaves*

– Sri Aurobindo

By the end of 1990 many non-governmental organisations (NGOs)
rose in prominence. Rajiv Gandhi's inclusion of a chapter in the
Plan document on the voluntary sector was a kiss of death of
sorts. Much money was allocated to the sector and along with it
came corruption and lack of transparency. The rise of Council for
Advancement of People's Action and Rural Technology (CAPART)
and the Central Social Welfare Board as special agencies to provide
funds for the voluntary sector resulted in them becoming dens of

corruption. CAPART is now closed due to several complaints; it is in the mortuary awaiting revival. The Central Social Welfare Board is not far behind. How did this take place and how did the sector fail to keep its stables clean? The increasing funds being devoted by the government, as Prakash Karat, CPI(M) general secretary said, was "co-option by the state of the independent sector". Soon many NGOs got large amount of funds between 1985 and 1990. There was no monitoring or evaluation or even clear-cut criteria to grant funds to the NGOs. This resulted in fraudulent NGOs getting grants and showing no work or progress. Often the same NGOs were represented on government committees as well. However, Left groups had always felt that NGOs killed the spirit of revolution and were only good at band-aid; and in the long run did no good.

In 1985 Sanjit (Bunker) Roy and some of his Social Work and Research Centre (SWRC) chapters introduced a Code of Conduct through the People's Action for Development of India (PADI), a government agency then run by Ashok Jaitly, an energetic officer of the Indian Administrative Service. The code of conduct was laudable. NGOs needed to follow norms.

The draft code of conduct formulated by PADI (1985) runs as follows:

- A rural voluntary organisation shall function according to its bylaws, rules and regulations and other statutory provisions to which it is subject.
- The organisation shall regularly hold meetings of its General Body and its other organs as prescribed and issue the proceedings of the meetings as prescribed.
- The organisation shall have its accounts audited as prescribed and submit the auditor's statement of accounts to the authorities prescribed.

- The organisation shall ensure that all reports and returns that it is obliged to file under the laws of the land are duly submitted to the appropriate authorities.
- If the organisation receives foreign assistance, it shall register itself with the Ministry of Home Affairs under the Foreign Contribution (Regulation) Act 1976 and observe all rules prescribed thereunder.
- All officers and staff of the organisation shall maintain high standards of integrity. They shall ensure that the funds of the organisation are not used for their benefit or for the benefit of their relations and friends unless they are lawfully entitled to receive the benefits.
- No activity of the organisation shall be used to promote the commercial, business or political interests of its officers.
- No officer of an organisation shall be an officer of a political party.
- No person holding an elected office in Parliament, a state legislature or Panchayati Raj institution shall be an officer of a voluntary organisation. An officer who intends to contest such an election shall resign from his office in the voluntary organisation.
- Every officer and paid functionary of a voluntary organisation shall declare their personal assets to the organisation every year.
- Every officer and paid functionary of a voluntary organisation shall lead a simple lifestyle and shall not show any ostentation. There shall be no noticeable disparity in the standard of living and the emoluments of officers and staff of a voluntary organisation.
- The organisation shall make every effort to avoid all

exploitative practices in the conduct of its own activities and as far as possible shall abide by all laws regulating employment, wages, work schedule, etc., in respect of its employees and workers.

- An organisation working for rural development shall have a base in a rural area.

- A voluntary organisation shall have broadbased objectives serving the social and economic needs of, mainly, the weaker sections of the community.

- A voluntary organisation shall adopt simple, innovative and inexpensive means and methods of working.

- A voluntary organisation shall have dedication, flexibility, professional competence (regardless of whether workers have a formal degree) and organisational skills to implement programmes.

- A voluntary organisation shall be explicitly committed to secular socialist social and democratic concepts and methods of functioning.

- A voluntary organisation shall declare that it will adopt constitutional and non-violent means for rural development purposes.

- A voluntary organisation shall plan and implement anti-poverty and minimum needs programmes and other related activities designed to raise the awareness of people living below the poverty line and leading to an improvement in the quality of their lives.

However, the draft code of conduct was opposed by a large set of NGOs. Bunker Roy and his group said this was due to foreign funding and gross misappropriation of foreign funds. A large meeting was held in 1987 in the Indian Social Institute, Lodhi Road, New Delhi, where the document was torn to shreds and Bunker Roy lost his shirt literally. It was a good move to introduce accountability in the sector where the NGOs had started building assets disproportionate to their income; there was also the involvement of relatives in work and grant of undue favours. PADI was later merged with another agency called Council for the Advancement of Rural Technology (CART) and the joint entity called CAPART was created. The same CAPART was closed in 2012 due to rampant corruption and the Tata Institute of Social Science (TISS) was given the task of reorganising CAPART and making it functional. This was a tall order. Bunker Roy was ahead of his times when he said a code of conduct was critical.

There were cases in Andhra Pradesh of an agency called CROSS (Community Rural Orient Service Society) run by Mathew Kurian and AWARE (Action for Welfare and Awakening in Rural Environment) run by PKS Madhavan, which were shut due to diversion of funds to personal use. These are being investigated. Madhavan set up AWARE in 1975 with three staff members and adopted three tribal and Harijan villages. His contribution in the upliftment of tribals from the most backward Mahbubnagar district to the inaccessible forest tracts of Khammam district in Telangana is undisputed. Today AWARE has 1,300 staff on its rolls. It has a volunteer force of nearly 52,000 people and footprint in 6,000 villages in Andhra Pradesh, Odisha, Kerala, Karnataka and Uttar Pradesh. It has helped more than three lakh families, rehabilitated 15,000 bonded labourers, recovered 45,000 acres rightfully belonging to the poor and made 300 villages in Andhra prosperous and able to sustain development. Madhavan always modestly maintained that he is only "a link in the belt and not the buckle," in AWARE.

But despite being recognised as the messiah of tribals in Andhra Pradesh, Odisha, Karnataka and Uttar Pradesh, one of his baiters within AWARE alleges: "He is a changed person today. Many more skeletons could tumble out of his (Madhavan's) cupboard and the Dutch body's (Netherlands Organisation for International Development Cooperation or NOIDC) complaint could be just the tip of the iceberg." A man who always claimed he had only an old car gifted by his father, which had to be pushed 20 km for covering every 10 km, today has more than half-a-dozen vehicles.

Madhavan is also known to have organised high-flying trips for well-known journalists, jurists and bureaucrats to derive maximum publicity for AWARE. Says an employee: "By hobnobbing with influential bureaucrats and jurists, he thinks he can get a protective cover for his loot." According to another staffer, he allegedly hired a private aircraft for taking a noted columnist to AWARE's boat hospital near Khammam. The well-equipped hospital serves inaccessible hamlets along the Godavari. The government did apply some brakes on Madhavan's financial wizardry at one point. It restricted foreign donations to AWARE when former union minister S Jaipal Reddy (then a legislator from Mahbubnagar) raised questions in the assembly in 1978 about AWARE getting foreign aid.

Madhavan took to politics in 1994. He unsuccessfully contested from the Kalwakurthy assembly constituency as an independent. Says he: "As I failed to convince the then chief minister not to give a ticket to the sitting legislator, I took the extreme step of contesting. I contested as an individual and not as AWARE chair. None of my staff members were involved in election duty." But it was a shortlived attempt at a crossover.

Today, AWARE has an annual budget of ₹30 crore. Though one

source says that "the flow of funds stopped more than half a decade ago, ever since the government woke up to AWARE's activities," Madhavan maintains that "there are as many as six donors, including NOIDC." He says, in response to NOIDC charging him with misappropriation of funds: "One of them (the Interchurch Cooperative for Development Cooperation or ICCO) had engaged KPMG, an international accounting firm with headquarters in Holland, to go through our accounts. In their report, the engaged auditors wrote: 'Based on our review, nothing has come to our attention to suggest that AWARE might have misappropriated or misutilised funds of ICCO or Novib (now Oxfam Novib)'. How can only one firm find fault with AWARE while others have no complaints whatsoever?"

Meanwhile, unperturbed by the court proceedings, Madhavan is busy handling the affairs of a super-speciality cancer hospital he has helped set up in Malakpet, Greater Hyderabad. When he is not doing that, he is busy shuttling between Bhagwatipuram on the city's outskirts to his NGO headquarters. He seeks to complete a ₹7 crore dream project BLISS, a human resource development institute, for which the Osmania University has accorded recognition to run courses.

A similar case was filed by the home ministry against Mathew Kurian of CROSS for misappropriation of foreign money using two bank accounts. There are, however, many others involved in such transactions.

By the turn of the century, media reports on NGOs were increasingly probing. They ranged from misappropriation of funds to foreign junkets and developmental tourism for foreign donors in rural areas. CAPART also published a list of 700 NGOs blacklisted by them, on which an important NGO senior quipped: "How can the pot call the kettle black? Increased funding to the sector was turning the voluntary sector into a den of thieves." Many lamented, including Bunker Roy: "I knew there was a problem in the sector but never knew the extent of it."

In many ways the metamorphosis, from a modest, village-level, kurta-pyjama clad activist into a well-heeled, suited-booted, city slicker whose voice is heard in high places, mirrors the changing face of India's burgeoning voluntary sector. Once the preserve of the humble jholawallah, the third sector of the Indian economy is now teeming with smart men and women, armed with management degrees, laptops and huge funds generated by a liberalised and booming economy. As the state retreats in an era of privatisation, new generation NGOs have moved in to fill the vacuum, often doing what the government used to do in rural areas and urban slums or conducting advocacy programmes for policy interventions, even holding skill-building workshops to update small voluntary groups. Their activities are vast and varied and bear little resemblance to the sweetly charitable work of the silent, selfless grassroots workers of the 1970s and the 1980s.

The growth of the sector has been explosive in the past two decades, both in numbers and financial resources. First, the numbers. If the findings of a survey conducted by the Central Statistical Organisation (CSO) of the ministry of statistics in 2008 are to be believed, there are 3.3 million NGOs registered in India. In other words, there is an NGO for every 400 Indians. No other country boasts of such huge numbers in the third sector. However, this mind-boggling figure should be taken with a pinch of salt. Even the report acknowledges that many are probably defunct. But, as Sanjay Agarwal, a chartered accountant who works with several NGOs, said: "At least the CSO has tried to shine a light where there was darkness all these years. No one has ever tried to collate data on the voluntary sector."

The CSO report is a starting point and its data is revealing. It found that a big growth spurt has happened since 1991. Thirty per cent of the 3.3 million NGOs were registered in the 1990s and 45 per cent more came up after the year 2000. While religious organisations and charities were the most commonly registered societies before 1970, there was a phenomenal expansion in social service organisations after 1991—as much as a 40 per cent increase, according to the CSO report.

It is significant that the phenomenal expansion of the voluntary sector coincides with the opening up of the economy and its rapid growth. India changed as it privatised and globalised, and the changes saw NGOs blooming in thousands as the civil society matured and began asserting itself. Nothing underscores their growing influence more than enforcement of the Right to Information Act and the National Rural Employment Generation Act, both of which were products of pressure from civil society organisations.

Yet, despite such growth, there has been little or no effort to map the voluntary sector or streamline it for transparency. It remains opaque, with questionable accountability levels, leaving it vulnerable to scams and scandals and the inevitable suspicion about sources and utilisation of funds. Because of the lack of comprehensive data, estimates about the financial size of the sector vary. One figure is as high as ₹75,000 crore annually, but Rajesh Tandon, president of PRIA (Society for Participatory Research in Asia), a mega NGO that works with a host of smaller ones, puts the amount of money available to this sector at around ₹40,000 crore a year.

Most of the funding comes from domestic sources, of which

the government is the largest donor. However, foreign donations make up a significant portion of the financial resources available to NGOs. Unfortunately, here too, despite a Foreign Contributions Regulation Act, no authentic figures are available, underlining the laxity that prevails in this sector. Former home minister P Chidambaram told Parliament that the government recorded a figure of around ₹10,000 crore from foreign donations in 2013. He added that this figure was grossly undervalued because nearly half the NGOs registered to receive foreign aid had not reported contributions received over the years. In other words, he said, foreign funding of the NGO sector could be as high as ₹20,000 crore.

The confusion and lack of systems to track funds have tarnished the image of the voluntary sector, despite the good work that many of them do. As with every sector, there are good NGOs and bad NGOs. Unfortunately, the latter hog the headlines. Scams are a plenty, particularly when it comes to the disbursement of government money. The rural development ministry's main funding agency, which also happens to be the biggest government donor, CAPART, fell into disrepute because of the high level of corruption in the department. However, CAPART also did exemplary work with medicinal herbs and supported Darshan Shankar, a noted activist from western Maharashtra who set up the Academy of Development Sciences in Kashele near Karjat. Later, he established FLRHT (Foundation for Revitalisation of Local Health Traditions, Bangalore) to promote medicinal plants and also herbs to treat people. Barring a few such good ones, the bulk of the NGOs funded by CAPART turned to be corrupt and non-performing.

In 2001 the author carried out an exercise under the insistence of Dr NC Saxena, member of the NAC (National Advisory Council, a non-constitutional advisory body to the government of India under the United Progressive Alliance) member and then Secretary to the Planning Commission. It was a validation exercise and a possible rating model for the NGO sector to see who was good and bad. The report is with the Planning Commission. It says a possible methodology exists but the government monitoring mechanism has to be squeaky clean too. In interviews with the NGO seniors, I found that repeated dishonesty among officials dealing with NGOs, deals struck by monitoring officials and also petty clerks in added to the lack of accountability in the sector. A meeting was held in Delhi between NGO seniors, chartered accountants who work with the sector and other academics teaching social work. Many more consultations followed in Kolkata, Mumbai, Bhubaneswar, Guwahati, Bangalore and Hyderabad. It became more evident that the voluntary sector needed minimum standards for governance. The laws were not sufficient. It was earlier said that the last refuge of the scoundrel was politics and it was now felt that the last refuge of the politician was to start an NGO. The sector was in dire straits and the media continued to report on NGO scams. It was also said a foreign company sold its seed company in the US and laundered money to set up an NGO in India. However, the Ministry of Home Affairs continued its one-sided attitude to victimise good NGOs who opposed nuclear plants or mining companies and displacement.

Non-governmental organisations like Give India, SOSVA (Society for Service to Voluntary Agencies), HelpAge India, COVA (Confederation of Voluntary Associations), Childline and many others joined in the effort to create minimum standards of governance and financial accountability. The Tata Institute of Social Sciences joined too. The Voluntary Action Network India (VANI), a voluntary network supported, this process and gave much-needed logistic support. In 2004 the standards were accepted by about 2000 NGOs at a meeting at Gandhi Peace Foundation, New Delhi. This led to the birth of the Credibility Alliance. Today, they accredit NGOs and have popularised the minimum standards of governance and financial accountability. It is a small but significant step to clean the mess. It is an attempt at self-regulation. Another initiative called Guidestar India was registered, which is an online platform for NGOs to showcase the work. Verified information is made available in the public domain and necessary documents pertaining to the NGO are available in one place. The database covers about 5,000 NGOs in India.

Today there is a new forward-looking statute, the Companies Act 2013 after 12 years of debate; it replaces the old Act of 1956. The new Act was necessitated by the changed context globally and the large number of corporate scandals, whether Coalgate or 2G, and a growing trust deficit in the NGO sector in India. However, India has a long and rich history of close business involvement in social causes for national development. In India, CSR is known from ancient times as a social duty or charity, which has evolved through different ages to a broader concept. India has had a long tradition of corporate philanthropy, and industrial welfare has been in practice since the late 1800s. Historically, business philanthropy in India has resembled Western philanthropy in terms of being rooted in religious beliefs. Business practices in the 1900s, which could be termed socially responsible, took different forms: philanthropic donations to charity, service to the community, enhancing employee welfare and promoting religious conduct. While corporations may give funds to charitable or educational institutions and may promote them as great humanitarian deeds, they may simply be trying to buy goodwill. The ideology of CSR in the 1950s was primarily based on an assumption of the obligation of business to society. In the initial years there was little documentation of social responsibility initiatives in India. Since then there is growing realisation towards contribution to social activities globally with a desire to improve the immediate environment (Shinde, 2005). It has also been found that, to a growing degree, companies that pay genuine attention to the principles of socially responsible behavior are favoured by the public. As funds from foreign sources are declining, non-profits are looking to the new Companies Bill and the CSR commitment of 2 percent of profits as a new source of funds. However, many companies are demanding accreditation as they do not know the good and the bad. Many NGOs are joining this move to accredit them. VANI, a network of NGOs, has also come up with principles of good governance for voluntary agencies.

Whether funds are foreign or Indian, efforts at self-regulation are coming from within the sector, which is a good sign. The challenges within the sector are enormous. There is no ideological leader like Swami Vivekananda or Vinobha Bhave. There is also a feeling that the semi-bureaucratic form of the NGO is a hindrance and a mass organisation with no fixed centre is better. More such organisations have risen to prominence in the twenty-first century. The parent NGO begins the work and soon spins off into a mass-based membership organisation; they are then able to carry the struggle through nonviolent and different forms of mass action. The Narmada Bachao Andolan, Manavi Hakka Abhiyan, Beej Bachao Andolan and even the recent India Against Corruption movement are such non-profit models. These have built-in accountability and transparency. These issues will occupy centre stage in the age of the internet and instant reporting.

Chapter 6

RISE OF CIVIL SOCIETY IN
THE 21ST CENTURY

*"There is no Maoism in Gajapati district of Odisha—
how do you remove Maoism without firing a single
bullet?"*

– Naveen Patnaik, Chief Minister of Odisha

It is a hot day in Berhampur and Naveen Patnaik, Chief Minister
of Odisha, is inaugurating a tribal girls hostel in Mohana, Gajapati
district. He knows the work of a Catholic priest chased out by
his own church but who struggled across Odisha transforming
the lives of tribals. The story of PREM (People's Rural Education
Movement) in Odisha's southern district of Gajapati is a remarkable
one. Father Jacob Thundyil was a Catholic priest in the 1970s and
was removed by the Bishop of Cuttack for his radical theology.
Many were influenced by Paulo Freire, the radical theologian who
wrote *Pedagogy of the Oppressed*. PREM started in Mandiapalli,
Berhampur, and changed the lexicon of work in southern Odisha.
Soon, the priest had two mass-based organisations, the All Orissa
Tribal Union and the All Orissa Dalit Union. Jacob says: "PREM

is only a vehicle for transformation and only a means to an end."
After a severe difference of opinion with the Bishop of Berhampur,
PREM was registered in 1980 and was soon a force to reckon
with in Mohuda, Gajapati. They spread fast to Koraput and other
districts in southern Odisha.

Similarly, in Maharashtra, Anna Hazare was leading a movement
in Ahmadnagar district against the evils of society and corruption.
Vivek Pandit and Eknath Avadh, activists in Marathwada, led a
movement against bonded labour called Manavi Hakka Abhiyan,
releasing thousands of bonded labour especially from the Mang
and Mahar communities there. This was caste-based bondage and
many political leaders had bonded labour in their houses. Eknath
Avadh, a Dalit activist, was a bonded labour as a child and knows
the travails. He says: "Landlords have beaten me and raped our
women. But today we will not let them go scot free." Thousands of
cases were filed and the Supreme Court appointed PV Rajagopal
as Supreme Court Commissioner to release these bonded labour
across the country. Rajagopal, a noted Gandhian, was trained by
famous activist Subba Rao who was able to get many dreaded
Chambal dacoits to surrender and lead normal lives. Rajagopal
went on to form Ekta Parishad, another mass-based organisation,
in Madhya Pradesh and Chhattisgarh on the issues of jal, jangal,
jameen—water, forests and land. Bonded labour became a major
issue and spread quickly. Today, if there is no bonded labour it is
due to the work of the civil society.

Later, there were similar mass-based movements in the Narmada
Bachao Andolan and in Odisha against displacement by the steel
and mining plants. These led to the Kalinganagar and anti-Posco
agitations. PREM also challenged the Tatas who acquired large
tracts of fertile land near Gopalpur on Sea. The Tatas wanted the

fertile land for a steel plant. The agitation finally led to the Tatas withdrawing from Gopalpur as they did in Singur.

Civil society was rising in India and there were movements across the country. The characteristics common to all registered voluntary or non-governmental organisations in India are:

- They exist independent of the state
- They are self-governed, by a board of trustees or managing committee or a governing council comprising individuals who generally serve in a fiduciary capacity
- They produce benefits for others, generally outside the membership of the organisation
- They are non-profits in that they are prohibited from distributing a monetary residual to their members.

However, the mass movements that later led to the India Against Corruption movement and the Aam Aadmi Party were structurally different. Mass-based organisations broadly have no registration and governance tends to be loose. There are usually one or two non-governmental organisations (NGOs) behind them, like Parivartan run by Arvind Kejriwal and Vidhayak Sansad run by Vivek Pandit who was the force behind the Manavi Hakka Abhiyan in Maharastra. Strangely, they are all coalitions or fluid organisations with no hardcore centre. Mass movements begun by civil society, thus, can spiral out of proportion as they do not have a clear structure or single-point leadership.

It all started with the Paulo Freire (1921-1997) model which PREM's founding fathers followed. It became a model for radical movements. The Freire method of education seeks to provide an open forum to learners, teachers, and the community alike. It also provides for the development of skills and competencies to help communities exercise power. The method came to be known as liberatory education. It supports learning with empowerment as the intended outcome. Liberatory education links the problems of illiteracy with broader social and political problems. Armed with these methods, many NGOs began work across India. Institutional structures gave way to mass movements.

In old Madhya Pradesh and now Chhattisgarh, Rajagopal set about organising tribals. He set up an NGO called Prayog in a small village, Tilda, near Raipur from where it expanded across Chhattisgarh. In time he formed the Ekta Parishad, a mass-based organisation, to fight on jal, jangal, jameen (water, forest, land) as the main issues. The tribals were exploited largely on these issues, which led them to poverty. Much of the technique used was the Freirian form of education. Groups starting from Raipur began challenging the state in Chhattisgarh and Delhi that land be restored to them. Forest land was being encroached upon by vested interests reducing the tribals to paupers. The same story was being played on in the mining districts with corporate interests and public sector companies displacing them. The Ekta Parishad opposed this and resisted displacement. A long march began from Raipur to Delhi and was stopped at Agra. Jairam Ramesh, then Minister of Rural Development, met Rajagopal and Ekta Parishad leaders on the instructions of then Prime Minister Manmohan Singh. Ramesh negotiated an agreement that a land reform committee would be set up to provide permanent settlement on these issues. The issue is still unsettled although civil society demonstrated that it could bring the government to its knees. The power of the state thus continues to be challenged. More NGOs continued this trend in the twenty-first century but the foundations were laid around 1975 in the anti-Emergency agitation and the Jayaprakash Narayan Nav Nirman movement. These NGOs created the new revolution which we see around us. The Scheduled Tribes and Other Traditional Forest Dwellers (recognition of forest rights) Act is a result of a protracted struggle by NGO leaders like Rajagopal, Jacob and many others. The notification of the Forest Rights Act 2006 on 1 January 2008 paved the way to undo the historic injustice done to the tribals by the British who colonised forests and tribal land.

Agriculture was going through a crisis and farmers in Vidarbha were committing suicide. Vidarbha has since become the centre for many farmers' suicides. A major civil society organisation, the Vidarbha Jan Andolan Samiti (VJAS) founded by Kishor Tiwari, has been at the forefront of agitations for better farmers' policy. Tiwari criticises the government for its lopsided and anti-farmer policies which are killing them.

Having completed his engineering from Amravati, Tiwari joined the state electricity department in Chandrapur. He later joined a multinational corporation with an MBA degree. Kishor quit his job as Regional Manager in Toshbro, a Japanese biotech company, to fight for farmers' rights when Vidarbha farmers started to have a tough time. Suicides have now become a huge problem not only in Vidarbha but across India.

The VJAS has been monitoring suicides by farmers and providing rehabilitation support to their families. They have taken it up with the administration, judiciary, legislature, human rights bodies, and on international fora. In a region where more than 70 per cent of the population is backward, the VJAS has been taking up issues like malnutrition among tribals, and their right to food, education and drinking water.

In 2004 the VJAS filed a public interest litigation (PIL) petition on malnutrition deaths among the Kolam tribals in Amravati division. The court directed the administration to provide food grain and other necessities to the dying tribals. The Yavatmal tribals' demand for land rights was, thus, met. The VJAS is now seeking monthly support for farmers' widows, many of whom are in their 20s and 30s.

Kishor says there is massive corruption and huge anomalies in the implementation of special farm relief packages. He says that until 1999, farmers' suicides were unheard of in Vidarbha. The introduction of Bt cotton in 2004 triggered the suicides. "The cultivation cost jumped from ₹5,000 an acre to ₹10,000 an acre. At the same time, the state government withdrew the cotton bonus (₹500 a quintal advance normally tagged on to the minimum support price). As if on cue, the Bt cotton crop failed that year. This is when the suicides began," says Kishor.

Various relief packages were announced. First was the ₹1,075 crore Chief Minister's package in December 2005. Then there was the ₹3,750 crore Prime Minister's package on 1 July 2006 followed by a central loan waiver and a state loan waiver. "They allotted ₹2,800 crore from the PM's package to increase irrigation facilities. They gave the rest to banks as interest waiver. The farmers got nothing," says Kishor. Since then, Kishor has always fought government policy when he thinks it is wrong.

The debate on genetically modified (GM) food has been as deep as the one on agricultural distress and suicides. Vandana Shiva is a world-renowned scientist and environmentalist based in Dehra Dun, India. She is part of an effort to place the Universal Declaration of Human Rights within something larger—a declaration of rights for Planet Earth. Vandana Shiva's Navdanya began as a programme of the Research Foundation for Science, Technology and Ecology (RFSTE), a participatory research initiative she founded. RFSTE was to provide direction and support to environmental conservation.

Organisations like these are battling to save Indian agriculture from a bigger disaster. Vandana Shiva has been leading the fight against GM seed and GM crop. Her work on Bt cotton and GM food has polarised the debate in India and outside; she continues to fight the companies promoting GM seed in India. As indicated earlier, Navdanya continues as a movement to save seeds and protect the right of the farmer to indigenous genetic material.

Vandana Shiva and her band of dedicated activists spearheaded the famous Beej Bachao Andolan to save indigenous seeds and germplasm from being robbed by various interests operating in India. These seeds, by GM foods, are classified as intellectual property and their marketing has impoverished farmers, changed their cropping pattern and created indebtedness. This ultimately led to suicides not only in Vidarbha but even in agriculturally strong states like Punjab.

Rajendra Singh, India's waterman

As mentioned earlier, Rajendra Singh, another Magsaysay Award winner for his water harvesting work and rejuvenation of dry rivers, began his walk across the Ganga basin to bring attention to the dying river.

He also initiated a National Water March (Rashtriya Jal Yatra) on 23 December 2002 from Gandhi Samadhi, Rajghat, New Delhi, and covered 30 states, including 144 river basins, in 22 months. He organised five national water conferences during this yatra in different parts of India. The Rashtriya Jal Yatra was an attempt to share water-related concerns and mitigate the pain of the poor and the farmers. The yatra stressed that we should strive to link people to rivers rather than interlink rivers, which he thinks will be a disaster. The experiences of the yatra germinated into the form of Tarun Jal

Vidyapeeth. Currently, Rajendra Singh is focusing on a Save the River Mission. He is a member of the National River Ganga Basin Authority, formed under the chairmanship of the Prime Minister of India. Singh has formed a Ganga Jal Biradari in 11 states of the Ganga River Basin. He has organised a yatra from Gomukh to Ganga Sagar to save the river from pollution, excess exploitation and encroachment in the Ganga Basin. He has motivated several volunteers to protect the Ganga and its tributaries.

Baba Adhav and Hamal Panchayat

Named Man of the Year by *The Week* in 2008, Baba Adhav, born 1930, is a veteran trade unionist working with porters in Maharashtra. His sole mission now is to get the Bill for social security of unorganised workers passed in Parliament. The smiling demeanour and the punishing travel schedule this veteran trade union leader of hamals (porters) in Pune follows makes it difficult to believe that he has lived for years with loss of vision in one eye and recurring back pain.

Baba, as his followers call him, earned honour for his relentless pursuit of ensuring basic rights for the country's unorganised workers. Baba operates out of a modest office in the labyrinthine lanes of Pune's Bhavani Peth area and is busy with the nitty-gritty of a proposed nationwide coalition of social organisations to pursue parliamentarians on the Unorganised Sector Workers Social Security Bill, which was introduced in the Rajya Sabha in September 2007.

Campaigning for social security

Baba is working president of the National Campaign Committee on Unorganised Labour.

"The Bill is the result of a long struggle," he says recalling its culmination in a gathering of some 5,000 workers representing 20-odd unions and organisations outside Parliament on 13 August 2007, to press for introduction of the Bill.

"The workers came from Gujarat, Maharashtra, Odisha, Uttar Pradesh, Bihar, Madhya Pradesh and Delhi," says Baba who, along with 70 workers, travelled by motorcycle from Pune addressing several meetings en route to Delhi.

In Delhi, he and Ela Bhat of SEWA, Ahmedabad, led a delegation to Sonia Gandhi, met parliamentarians and got 60 eminent people, including writer Khushwant Singh, Supreme Court lawyer Indira Jaising, human rights activist Swami Agnivesh, economist and former minister Yogendra K Alagh, actor and social activist Shabana Azmi and historian Ramachandra Guha to sign a petition in support of the legislation.

For Baba, this legislation could be the logical conclusion of his five-decade-long struggle for the country's most exploited people, whether working in the urban industry and commerce or toiling on rural farms.

What especially angers him is political apathy. "After generations of service, unorganised (sector) workers have little or no livelihood security. They do not get paid for days they are sick, nor is there compensation if they break their backs. Still, what should constitute social security legislation baffles many including our parliamentarians. Sometimes I wonder whether our elected representatives are merely ignorant or adopting a deliberate strategy," he says.

Of the 40 crore workers in India, less than 2.5 crore are protected by some form of labour legislation. They enjoy work security, minimum wages, an eight-hour working day, a weekly off, paid leave, sick leave, annual bonus, provident fund, pension and so on. The remaining 37.5 crore workers have been ignored. These include porters, headloaders, landless labourers, construction workers, domestic workers, brick kiln workers, quarry workers, cycle rickshaw pullers, waste-pickers, hawkers and vendors.

"We Indians do not value manual work. There is strange prejudice against it, especially among the white collared sections. We seem to forget that the domestic workers who serve us, the roadside vendors who provide for our daily needs, the construction workers who build our high-rises, and the waste-pickers who help keep our cities clean are as much a part of modern India as the information technologists and technocrats," he says.

Initial involvement

Baba's Hamal Panchayat, a trade union movement launched in 1955, has demonstrated that the work conditions of unorganised workers can be improved only through a rights-based struggle for dignity and against exploitation, backed by supportive legislation. Baba Adhav became involved with the issues of hamals and mathadis (headloaders) in Pune's markets in the early 1950s, as a young practising doctor. Born and brought up in Pune's old Peth area, Baba grew up watching the daily toil in the timber, grain and metal markets. He was a committed Seva Dal activist, inducted into its shakha (unit) and introduced to socialist ideals as a schoolboy.

Baba's earliest activity was running a news board on street corners where the hamals would gather after a hard day's work. This helped him consolidate the hamals' support and understand their working conditions. At that time there was little or no information about the employment of hamals, though they were as good as permanent employees.

"The Shops and Establishments Act of 1948 did not require

hamals to be on the employment rolls of business establishments. This meant that they were not eligible for various benefits, nor would they have legal recourse should they be treated unfairly," recalls Baba.

On 19 November 1956, the Hamal Panchayat in Pune struck work for the first time over the issue of denial of wage hikes by jaggery merchants to hamals. The four-day strike was a success, and the porters realised the power of the trade union.

In 1962, the panchayat sought a law to protect the rights of the unorganised porters. It was a long struggle before the Maharashtra Mathadi, Hamal and other Manual Workers (Regulation of Employment and Welfare) Act was passed in 1969.

Through this landmark legislation, hamals were, for the first time, recognised as workers engaged in regular employment and entitled to all the privileges and benefits of permanent workers.

"But due to pressure from the trader lobby, neither the government nor the labour department was keen on it. It was only in 1974 that its implementation began in Pune, Mumbai and Nagpur. It was only after Supreme Court orders in 1980 that almost all the zillas started serving notices across the state. Nonetheless, almost 300,000 hamals are protected under this Act and benefit from it in Maharashtra," says Baba.

Baba also served as a councillor in the Pune Municipal Corporation for 10 years but quit active politics in 1971. Since then he has played a major role in pursuing the state authorities to enact progressive legislation like the Slum Rehabilitation Act, Dam and Project-Affected Rehabilitation Act, and the Devdasi Rehabilitation Act, besides the Mathadi Act.

"In my younger days I was quite adventurous. That is how I lost one eye," says Baba with a twinkle in his eye.

In 1963, he along with Datta Deshmukh and Jaisingh Mali, floated the Maharashtra Rajya Dharan ani Prakalpgrasta Shetkari Punarvasan Parishad, an association of displaced farmers and project-affected persons.

Baba was at the forefront of all satyagrahas against irrigation projects in the Krishna river valley and, on one occasion, flung himself in front of the passing car of former Chief Minister Yashwantrao Chavan, injuring himself and damaging one eye permanently.

Baba has served nearly 50 prison terms during the many agitations he has spearheaded over the years. The longest term was a year and-a-half during the Emergency.

Spirit of sharing

Baba's work though has not been limited to agitations and confrontations. He is a firm believer in dialogue, awareness and welfare of the unorganised. The Hamal Panchayat's Kashtachi Bhakar, a community kitchen for the poor and marginalised in Pune, epitomises the spirit of giving, sharing and building that he has nurtured among his followers.

Started as a small kitchen in 1974, the Kashtachi Bhakar aimed to provide basic nutritious food to less privileged sections of society on a no-profit-no-loss principle.

A full meal of vegetables, roti, rice, vegetable and dessert costs barely ₹15 per person, while cheaper options like roti-vegetable or jhunka-bhakar are available for as little as ₹6-7.

This venture has thrived over the past three decades and today has 13 outlets feeding around 15,000 people every day and employing 50 men and 53 women, all from marginalised sections of society.

"After exerting themselves physically all day, food is what hamals need the most. To reduce the pain of hunger and exertion, many hamals are known to take to tobacco or drinking and, in turn, their families have to also go hungry. So the basic idea is to provide fresh, healthy and affordable food not only to hamals but to all the poor people of the city," says Baba.

Aruna Roy and Bunker Roy

In 1965 a young post-graduate student, Sanjit 'Bunker' Roy volunteered to spend the summer working with famine affected people in Palamu district of Bihar, now in Jharkhand, one of the poorest of India's states. His urban elitist upbringing had distanced him from poverty and destitution. This experience changed him, and formed the determination to fight poverty and inequality. It became his mission. The idea of the Social Work and Research Centre (SWRC), Tilonia, emerged from these concerns. There was no fixed agenda.

In the late 1960s, a small group of determined educated youth started looking for alternative ways of addressing poverty in rural India. This search for working models, approaches and strategies led some of them to live and work in villages.

The answer seemed to lie in beginning a dialogue between the specialist and the farmer in a relationship born of equality and respect. In 1972, Meghraj from Tilonia village and Bunker Roy a became friends and shared a dream grafting formal urban knowledge on rural wisdom to create a world without want. Anil Bordia the then collector of Ajmer helped lease an abandoned Tuberculosis Sanatorium premises from the government at ₹1 a month, in Tilonia.

In the beginning the professionals were geologists, economists, doctors, social workers, chartered accountants, graduates and post-graduates who came to share this dream with concerned villagers. While questioning the system's sluggish delivery of promised basic services, assumptions of technological competence in development programmes were also challenged. For instance, did you need an engineer to repair a hand pump? Cannot midwives be trained to literally deliver better? Could not the rich traditional folk art and music be used for development communication? Instead of training women for leadership, could we not identify strong leaders to facilitate their learning about legal and other constitutional rights? Empowering them to question social oppression, the most difficult to confront in society?

Bunker Roy was influential in starting a new set of activists, and his spouse Aruna Roy continued to fight this oppression in Rajasthan. In the late 1990s Aruna Roy visited various rural works in Rajasthan where many labourers were unpaid and sometimes underpaid. Public works had become a big source of corruption. Aruna Roy founded the Mazdoor Kisan Shakti Sanghatan (MKSS), a grassroots organisation, in 1990. It works in rural Rajasthan with a stated objective of using modes of struggle and constructive action to change the lives of the rural poor. In the period leading up to its formation, it had taken up issues of redistribution of land and minimum wages. These were seen as the two basic issues of the rural landless and the poor of the area. To understand why the demand for minimum wages and the subsequent demand for access to records came about, it is important to get a sense of the geographical and sociopolitical setup of the area where the MKSS works. Rajasthan being a desert state, the people are faced more often than not with drought. When the rains fail, the only choice is to either migrate or be employed at famine relief work sites. A famine relief site is basically a work site opened by the government to provide employment. This could be building a road, digging a well or desilting ponds and lakes. Women outnumber men in most of these work sites. Men tend to migrate in search of livelihood and the women are left behind to tend the family.

It was seen initially that the labourers at the famine relief sites were not paid full minimum wage. When they demanded to be paid minimum wages on public works, they were refused on the grounds that "they did not work." When the labourers questioned the authorities, they were told the records showed they did not work. The records in question were "measurement books" filled by a Junior Engineer. The labourers then demanded to see the records. The administrators told them they could not see the records; according to the Official Secrets Act (1923), a colonial legacy, these records were state secrets and could not be opened up to the public. This infuriated the labourers who then said, "till we get access to those records, we will always be told that we don't work and the administration can never be challenged on that account. If we are to prove what they say is not true we need to get those records."

It was at this point that the movement for right to information began. The need to access records was established and people began to think of how they could get the government to give them the right to know. The modes adopted were diverse; an important aspect was that people identified totally with the cause. For them it was their battle, a battle for survival. The struggle illustrated that the right to information was not just a component of people's right to freedom of speech and expression, but was also a part of their fundamental right under Article 21 of the Constitution the right to life and liberty. The villagers understood, and made a large section of enlightened opinion in India understand, that access to records of development work in villages would help obtain basic living wage, entitlement under the ration quota, the medicines the poor should receive in public health centres, prevent abuse by the police, and even prevent delay and subterfuge in implementation of other livelihood entitlements. A number of slogans that the MKSS used in various phases came from the understanding of this struggle. Slogans such as "our money, our account", "the right to know, the right to live", "this government belongs to you and me, it's no one's personal property."

In demanding a law for the right to information, people established their desire to be part of the democratic framework in which they would be given a fair hearing and their views would be taken into consideration while forming policies. The goal was to establish the concept of participatory democracy, to make the governors understand that the common man now wanted a share in governance.

The MKSS adopted many strategies to achieve these goals. These included sit-ins, rallies, and lobbying with government. Culture and innovative ways of communication were also used through music, puppets and street theatre.

When the initial phase of agitation began with a sit-in, the government of Rajasthan reluctantly passed an order (after much pressure) whereby people were given the right to inspect records and later to get certified photocopies. At the time of inspecting the records of a village council, the MKSS found many irregularities and malpractices. From this emerged the technique of the public hearing which has been used as a tool to uncover many scams.

Usually, in a public hearing, the MKSS first obtains the records pertaining to public works carried out by a village council in the past five years. Once the documents are accessed, the MKSS takes the records to each village where the work is said to have been executed.

Testimonies are sought from the villagers and the labourers who were employed on the site. The MKSS also does site verification with the labourers and villagers. On the day of the public hearing, in front of the general assembly of the villagers, details are read out and testimonies sought. There is also a panel of people invited to the public hearings, including lawyers, journalists, academicians and government officials. The panel is allowed to cross-examine, and with the administration present, attempts are made to bring about corrective measures for the irregularities identified. The malpractices usually uncovered are purchase overbilling, sale overbilling, fake labour rolls, underpayment of wages and in some cases ghost works (works that are on record but do not exist).

In many cases it has been seen that a public hearing causes rapid escalation in payments. People who haven't been paid for years, and have been denied payment after repeated visits to a Sarpanch (elected village council representative), all of a sudden find them being paid overnight. What is more, in many cases a Sarpanch comes to a labourer and pays him, adding that now that the payment has been made there is no need for them to testify at the public hearing. There have also been cases where, after the public hearing and embezzlement being proved, a Sarpanch has paid back the amount into the panchayat exchequer. Action has been initiated against officials found to be in compliance with acts of embezzlement.

The public hearing has been an effective tool in bringing to light corrupt practices and in trying to fix the leakages within the system. The strength also lies in the truth that emerges in front of people and their willingness to testify against a person in power, who often belongs to a higher caste and has a social standing that can be intimidating. The battle for rights and the fact that people, irrespective of gender, are willing to testify against those in power shows great potential in public hearings. One of the biggest legacies of Aruna Roy and the MKSS is the Right to Information Act commonly known as the RTI. This Act has given a tool to many including Aam Aadmi Party leader Arvind Kejriwal who started activism on the RTI with an organisation called Parivartan.

Many activists gravitated towards a tool now rearing its head and empowering India's citizens like no other tool has—the RTI Act, a law that entitles a citizen to get information from the government. Aruna Roy, Harsh Mander, Nikhil Dey and many others met at the Lal Bahadur Shastri Academy, a premier institute for training India's bureaucrats, actively supported by the Director Dr NC Saxena, and drafted the initial bill. She ultimately won the Magsaysay Award for this landmark bill freeing Indians from the British legacy of the Official Secrets Act. Civil society has given the RTI to India. It has also given the Unorganised Workers Bill and the Forest Protection Act.

Civil society has in the twenty-first century brought the rights agenda to the public domain. Many bills pertaining to people's rights have been passed—from the RTI to a basic fundamental necessity such as the right to food. Implementation in many states however remains tardy and ineffective. The political will to implement the rights seems to be missing. The missionary zeal of non-profits has brought these bills to Parliament. Democracy is moving forward and enlarging their scope. However, civil society is also changing its institutional character. The typical jholawalas (activists with a sling bag called the jhola) have now moved centrestage into the political domain. The Aam Aadmi Party has its fair share of civil society activists. However, there are many who will continue to say they are not accountable.

Civil society leaders like Rajendra Singh, Rajagopal, Jacob, Kishor Tiwari, Baba Adhav, Bunker and Aruna Roy have challenged the boundaries of their mission. They have led movements that enlarged democracy and gave people their rights. Nobody can deny their contribution to India. Civil society has been actively pursuing the Mahatma's goal set in Wardha in 1948. Although a fanatic's bullet stopped him, his spirit continues to influence India on its million missions. The Father of the Nation would have been proud.

WORKS CITED

Introduction

1) Rajesh Tandon & SS Srivastava, *Invisible, Yet Widespread: The Non-profit Sector in India*, (New Delhi: PRIA, 2002). The study was conducted in collaboration with the Institute for Policy Studies, John Hopkins University, Baltimore, USA.

Chapter 1

1) Rajesh Tandon & SS Srivastava, *Invisible, Yet Widespread: The Non-profit Sector in India*, (New Delhi: PRIA, 2002). The study was conducted in collaboration with the Institute for Policy Studies, John Hopkins University, Baltimore, USA.

2) Final report on "Non-profit Institutions in India—A Profile and Satellite Accounts in the framework of System of National Accounts (including State-wise Comparison of Profiles)" by National Accounts Division, Central Statistics Office, Ministry of Statistics and Programme Implementation, Government of India, March 2012.

Chapter 2

1) Klaus K Klostermaier, *Hinduism: A short introduction* (Oneworld Publications, 2000).

Chapter 3

1) His Holiness the Dalai Lama and Howard C Cutler MD, *The Art of Happiness in a Troubled World* (New York: Doubleday Religion, 2009).

2) Mathew Cherian and Anil Singh, "Dimensions of the voluntary sector", a Charities Aid Foundation Voluntary Action Network of India (CAF-VANI) publication, 2001.

3) Pushpa Sundar, *A study of giving in India*, (New Delhi: Indian Centre for Philanthropy, Sampradaan, 2001).

Chapter 4

1) Hazel Anderson, "Changing the game of finance", paper presented at "The World as We Want It to Be" SRI in the Rockies 20th Anniversary, October 25-28, 2009, http://www.ethical markets.com/2009/10/15/changing the game of finance/

2) Anil Agarwal and Sunita Narain, *Towards Green Villages: A Strategy for Environmentally—Sound and Participatory Rural Development* (New Delhi: Centre for Science and Environment, 1989).

3) Anil Agarwal, Ravi Chopra and Kalpana Sharma, *The State of India's Environment—1982: A Citizens' Report* (New Delhi: Centre for Science and Environment, 1982).

4) Anil Agarwal and Sunita Narain, *The State of India's Environment 1984-85: A Second Citizens' Report* (New Delhi: Centre for Science and Environment, 1985).

Chapter 5

1) Sri Aurobindo, *Towards holistic management* (Pondicherry: Sri Aurobindo Society, 2004).
2) Shivani Shinde, "Social responsibility corporate style", 2005, http://computer.financialexpress.com/20050502/technologylife01.shtml

GLOSSARY

Alimiyat:	graduation
Amilun:	collects and distributes
Amir:	chairperson
Anna daan:	gifting food
Balwadi:	pre-school run in rural areas run by government/ non-governmental organisations
Bhaber:	wild grass used for rope-making
Bhajans:	spiritual songs
Chadhawa:	offerings
Daan, daana, daanam:	the act of giving.
Dasvandh:	giving a tenth of one's income for the poor and disabled in Sikhism.
Desh kaal and patra:	place, time and person
Dharamshalas:	rest houses
Din:	religion
Fazilat:	post graduation
Fidiya:	fine imposed for violating fast during Ramadan
Fiqh:	understanding of jurisprudence
Fitrah:	religious giving
Fuquar:	poor

Garimun:	debtors
Gyan daan:	gifting knowledge
Hiba:	gifts
Iftar:	breaking the fast during month of Ramadan
Imamat:	religious leadership
Jaziya:	per-capita tax levied on an Islamic state's non-Muslim subjects
Khilafat:	succession
Langar:	feast
Mahila mandal:	women's group
Masakin:	the needy
Mohtamim:	principal
Motarnad-i-maliyat:	treasurer
Motarnad-i-talim:	academic advisor
Muftis:	legists, experts on law
Mungeri:	a valuable Indian fibre grass
Musafir khana:	rest house for the traveller
Muttawali:	caretaker
Nar seva, narayanseva:	service to mankind is service to God
Nazim:	secretary general
Nazrana:	offerings
Nisab:	syllabus
Nizan:	management
Qazis:	judges
Riqab:	ransom for captives
Sabhas, anjumans, samajes:	gatherings
Sadqah/Sidq:	truth
Sanatan dharma:	original name of Hinduism
Sanghas:	groups
Sanskara:	personal sacraments traditionally observed in every stage of life

Glossary

Shakhas:	branches
Shram daan:	gifting one's labour
Shura:	consensus through consultation
Taknik:	doctorate
Ulema:	Muslim legal scholars engaged in several fields of Islamic studies
Umma:	the community
Ushar:	agricultural produce
Vairagya:	detachment
Vastra daan:	gifting clothes
Vidya daan:	gifting knowledge
Wakf:	donation to a charitable trust
Waqif:	a person making donation
Yajna:	worship of divinity
Zakat:	portion of person's income reserved for charity in Islam

ABOUT THE AUTHOR

Mathew Cherian is Chief Executive, HelpAge India, a leading advocacy and caregiver non-profit for the elderly. He is based out of New Delhi, India, and has been associated with many non-profit groups across India and the world. He is an engineering graduate from the Birla Institute of Technology and Science (BITS), Pilani. He is among India's first rural managers from the Institute of Rural Management, Anand (IRMA) in Gujarat. He has been Director, Oxfam, in India and Executive Director, Charities Aid Foundation. His most recent initiative was in the establishment of Credibility Alliance, which works towards establishing accountability and transparency in civil society.

He is currently on the boards of HelpAge International, Guidestar International, Care International and Sightsavers, all well-known non-profit organisations. He is member of the National Council of Senior Citizens and the National Foundation for Communal Harmony. He is currently the Independent Commissioner for Geriatric Health with the government of India's Ministry of Health and Family Welfare. Amita Joseph is his partner; they have two daughters Aparajita and Arundati who helped greatly in writing this book.